NEW PLAYS
FROM A.C.T.'S
YOUNG CONSERVATORY

CRAIG SLAIGHT is the Director of the Young
Conservatory at the American Conservatory
Theater in San Francisco. Prior to joining A.C.T.,
Mr. Slaight was head of the acting and directing
program at the Los Angeles County High School
for the Arts. He also served on the theater faculty at
the Interlochen Center for the Arts. In addition to
his commitment to developing and training young
actors, Mr. Slaight spent ten years in Los Angeles
as a professional director. He currently serves on
the Territorial Board of the Educational Theatre
Association and is a member of the Theater Panel
for ARTS, sponsored by the National Foundation
for Advancement in the Arts. He is co-editor (with
Jack Sharrar) of *Great Scenes for Young Actors
from the Stage* and *Great Monologues for Young
Actors*.

i

The Young Conservatory at American Conservatory Theater

A.C.T.'s Young Conservatory is a professional theater training program for young people ages 8 to 18. The emphasis is on the training of an actor and the development of a young person in relationship to their world and to others. The program provides quality theater training for the beginner, exploring theater and acting for the first time, as well as advanced level study for the young person with provious experience. Classes are designed to develop imagination, concentration, working with others, exploration of character, development of technique in acting, and skills of both the body and the voice. Learning to respect people and the creative process are essentials in the program. Some students come to explore and discover, others come to define and refine their talent and technique to take them further in their goal to become a professional actor. The faculty are working theater professionals who are passionate and skilled in their working with young actors. The Young Conservatory seeks to empower young people to strive for excellence in their lives, while embracing an atmosphere of safety that encourages exploration. The training opportunities frequently extend students the opportunity to play the young roles in the professional company, learning firsthand from working artists.. The Young Conservatory is particularly devoted to developing in young people an appreciation of Theater in the making of a more human world, and in the importance of the place young people have in the future of the American Theater. To this end, the Young conservatory is a center for actor training for young people and development of new theater writing both by young people and by professional playwrights challenged to see the world through the eyes of the young. Critical thinking, feeling, and giving are cornerstones of this twenty year program.

Other Books in
The Young Actor Series
from Smith and Kraus

Great Monologues for Young Actors

Great Scenes for Young Actors from the Stage

Scenes and Monologues for the Very Young

Monologues From Classic Plays

Scenes from Around the World

Monologues from Around the World

17 Short Plays by Romulus Linney

If you require pre-publication information about upcoming Smith and Kraus monologue collections, scene collections, play anthologies, and advanced acting books, you may receive our semi-annual catalogue, free of charge, by sending your name and address to Smith and Kraus Catalogue, P.O. Box 10, Newbury, VT 05051.

NEW PLAYS
FROM A.C.T.'S
YOUNG CONSERVATORY

Edited by
Craig Slaight

The Young Actors Series

SK
A Smith and Kraus Book

A Smith and Kraus Book
Published by Smith and Kraus, Inc.

Cover and text design by Julia Hill
Manufactured in the United States of America

First Edition: February 1993
10 9 8 7 6 5 4 3 2 1

Publisher's Cataloging in Publication
Prepared by Quality Books

New plays from A.C.T.'s Young Conservatory / Craig Slaight.
p. cm.
Audience: Ages 12-22
ISBN 1-880399-25-3

1. American drama--Collections. 2. Plays--Collections. I.
Slaight, Craig. II. American Conservatory Theatre. III. Title:
New Plays from American Conservatory Theatre's Young
Conservatory.

PS625.5.N49 1993   812'.5400835
                                     QBI93-20017

Smith and Kraus, Inc.
Main Street, P.O. Box 10, Newbury, Vermont 05051
(802) 866 5423

ACKNOWLEDGEMENTS

The editor wishes to thank Carey Perloff, John Sullivan, Susan Stauter, Jack Sharrar, Maureen McKibben, Judy Johnson Wilson, Michele Bernier, Dennis Powers, Richard Butterfield, Jonathan Marks, Teddy Schley, Helen Palmer, Peter Franklin, Gilbert Parker, Mary Harden, and the staff and students of the American Conservatory Theater, for assisting in the creation of this new body of work. Special grateful thanks go to Smith and Kraus who continue to demonstrate their belief in the journey of young actors by publishing these books.

For
Edward Hastings
and
Horton Foote
two heroes
who have inspired courage.

CONTENTS

A Youthful Challenge
By Craig Slaight

If you are a young actor, or if you work with young actors, you have discovered that the search for plays suitable for performance and for study is a task that is unending. It is often a task that is limited to what has been most popularly produced by and for young people in recent years. Finding good plays has lead theater artists through centuries of explorations considering the great classics of times past as well as trends and styles of current plays.

Whether it is a current play or a classic, there is a wonderful opportunity to explore the journey of youth in the theater since the theater is a place where all of life is worthy of such exploration. The theater doesn't discriminate. At its best, the theater reflects an ageless truth. Young people often don't realize that the theatre is, as Arthur Miller once called it, a "hall of jurisprudence." The theater is a place where we can wrestle with important life experiences. These experiences aren't only adult experiences. Since adults produce theater and make up the largest audience to attend the theater, many plays deal with adult life. For young people, perhaps without realizing it, there doesn't appear to be a challenge. It seems that the voice of the young is often unheard in the theater. This doesn't have to be the case.

There is an essential and compelling value in witnessing the journey of youth. Adults are offered the opportunity to reexamine the turns life has presented them and bring a new perspective to their lives. Young people can learn first hand that the theater is a place where their life can be explored, now, just as significantly as when they are older. If we grow in this exploration, if we stretch our capacity to feel, to understand, to change, then the theater event has value. This doesn't end when we leave the theater, but can continue to ripple throughout our lives. The possibility of startling ideas and thoughts, offered in a light that is bigger than life, even as it is mirroring that life, is the essence of what makes the theater such a joyous art. If you are learning about being an actor in such a theater, or if you work with young people taking this acting journey, you must hunger to read and see plays constantly. This hunger is instinctual and insatiable to those of us who call the theater our home.

At the American Conservatory Theater, our two-fold mission to produce fine theater and train actors involves this ageless embrace: making the theater a place for all of life's experiences to be dealt with; all ages, all worlds, all beliefs. Our training programs offer a place for the young and the old to meet. Our youngest actor is eight. Senior members of our company are in their seventies. Being charged to lead the Young Conservatory (actors training between the ages of eight and eighteen), I feel compelled to explore the life journey of young people. This means, in part, finding plays that have this perspective on life, but plays that are also well written, well crafted, and hold themselves up as examples of fine drama to the young actors who want to learn fine acting. Admittedly, this quest for quality dramatic literature that is seen through the eyes of the young, presents an exciting opportunity and a challenge. Where does one look for these plays?

To begin with, one searches through the classics to find the age-old but ageless values, themes, ideas, language, and experiences. Great plays have dealt with the experience of youth. *Antigone* struggled with an adult world for her integrity. The fate of the star-crossed lovers in Shakespeare's *Romeo and Juliet* continues to haunt our lives. Eugene O'Neill's beautiful *Ah! Wilderness* provides a look at the world through the eyes of a young man coming of age, in his relationship to the world beyond his immediate existence, and in his struggle to know what truth means in his life. In addition, one reads as many new plays as possible to find the voices of today. Some programs even offer the playwrighting pen to young people to apply their perspective on life in a theatrical venue. All of these methods yield exciting possibilities for young people and are worthy explorations. It is my feeling, working with young actors in a vital theater like A.C.T., that perhaps we have another opportunity, one that serves our training mandate, and one that also contributes to the world of the theater.

Directing plays professionally, I've had the opportunity to work with a number of playwrights. For me, the playwright is the true muse of the theater. From making marks on paper we can suddenly experience life's richest and most perplexing moments. Anyone who can do that is in my book of amazing wonder-makers. The playwright is at the center of the theater, leading us all in the ideas and feelings that we wrestle with on stage. As director, I've always felt my job was to illuminate the page, to interpret the truth as told in the play, to give it form and beauty. Often playwrights will choose to see the world through youthful eyes, creating an ageless moment in time that brings old and young together in a glimpse of life. This interested me very much. Here we were in a theater where all these ages live together in their work, the younger learning from the more seasoned the craft and the spirit of creating art. I said to myself, "Where better could we challenge America's fine playwrights to write new plays with a perspective of youthful experience than at A.C.T., where this challenge goes on all the time between young and old?" It is fortunate that A.C.T. is the kind of place where such explorations are embraced with enthusiasm. Since A.C.T. has a history as a center for producing quality theater and training, I felt our institution, behaving very uninstitution-like, just might be a home for a playwright's new play, born in an atmosphere of creating without demanding a commercial success. Perhaps by mixing a play that was still in evolution with young actors who were learning their craft, and a professional playwright and director, we might enhance our training experience, stimulate the professionals, and give birth to a new play that could have a life for many years to come. But who would understand the need for this kind of work? Who would wish to accept our challenge to "see the world through the eyes of the young?"

Timothy Mason was the first person I approached. We had worked together on a professional production of his play *Levitation* and I knew him to be a wonderful playwright and someone who had written for young people in children's theater. When I offered him the challenge to write this kind of play he immediately said "yes." He added, "I'm excited to be asked to write this play and terrified." "Why terrified?" I asked. He went on to say, "I'm always terrified when I know that there will be a new play to write." I paused. "It's alright, terrified is good" was Tim's reply. So we began.

It was several months later that I received a telephone call from Tim saying he had just driven from Minneapolis to his home in New York when the idea of the play came to him. As he drove past a lake, loons lamenting in the water, he thought of two characters from another play he was developing, *The Fiery Furnace*. That play explores the relationship of three women, a mother and two sisters, whose lives have come to a peak--a dangerous place for all of them. Tim wondered what this life had been like when the two sisters were younger. What was the seed in youth that lead to these troubles later in life? A camp setting, years ago, and these two sisters came to him as the genesis for a new play about young people. He was on his way to creating *Ascension Day*. He applied this "journey of youth" challenge to his artistic scope on life and began to feel a new child being born. I recall the telephone conversation ended with Timothy reading a few lines from his notebook. I'm quite sure those lines, in one form or another, are in *Ascension Day*.

A short two months after that call I had the pleasure of sitting in a studio at the O'Neill Theater Center, in Waterford, Connecticut, and hearing *Ascension Day* read for the very first time, ever. It was a beautiful, disturbing play and I knew that we had been right to ask this gifted man to be our first commission. Although the characters in the play are teenagers, the reading at the O'Neill featured college-aged actors. I remember remarking to Tim that he had captured the voice of young people so well but I knew he would be amazed at the difference in the sound of his words when spoken by actors the same age as the characters--teenagers. At our first rehearsal in San Francisco, Tim agreed that the voices were strikingly different. In fact, he was concerned that perhaps he had written words and situations that were outside the life experiences of these actors. He found the complete opposite to be true.

At the Young Conservatory we work three days a week for five weeks on the new plays. The playwright is invited to attend all rehearsals, insisting that they be with us for at least two of the five weeks. Timothy Mason was able to be with us the entire time. His initial instinct was to come and go during the process. He became so fascinated with the actors, however, that he literally attended all rehearsals. The actors in turn were thrilled to actually have the playwright with us. He was our first resident playwright! This provided a wonderful opportunity for professional and young actor to interface. They became instant companions in art.

Tim delivered a completed draft of the play six weeks prior to our first rehearsal. Although set in 1947, *Ascension Day* seemed so immediate to the young actors. The universality of the themes, the relationships between the characters, the troubling situations presented in the play all seemed truthful to them. During the rehearsals Tim would adjust phrases, change words, supply ideas and comments to both the director and to the actors. Based on what he was seeing develop in rehearsal, he expanded the play with two additional scenes. Actors, director, and playwright were engaged in lively discussions, all of which contributed to the excitement of the project and propelled us forward. Clearly something exciting was happening! The audiences were genuinely moved by Timothy Mason's play and by the passion with which the young actors delivered it.

Mary Gallagher's *Windshook* was a thrilling, albeit different, experience. Like Timothy Mason, Mary was eager to accept the challenge. She knew A.C.T., having been with the company in the mid 1970's with two of her plays in the Plays-In-Progress program (a developmental venue for playwrights to try out their new scripts). She felt that this new approach with young actors would be a wonderful opportunity to have an A.C.T. reunion of sorts. Mary's idea for *Windshook* came from an old Scottish ballad that was a favorite, " The Mill o' Tifty's Annie". The song concerns a young girl who is considered the prettiest girl in the land. The family wants Annie to use her beauty to secure them a higher social standing: if she marries the Lord of the land (who's taken by her beauty), she will elevate the family's status and bring them riches. Annie, however, falls in love with the Lord's trumpetera common man. Against her family's wishes, she devotes herself to the trumpeter. Finally, she's beaten to death by the jealous brother. Mary was moved by this powerful story of youthful love, ambition, and rage. She was also moved by the contemporary issues facing the people who live in her part of the country. An economically depressed mountain area, near a big city, is where she placed *Windshook*. The Persian Gulf War had just ended and she used the pressures of the current world situation to explore a family at odds with each other and a mysterious visitor who changes their lives.

Mary had completed only twenty pages of what would be a seventy page script by the time we were ready to start rehearsals. After lengthy talks with her and grasping a sense of the characters in the early pages, we cast the play and set out at the beginning of this new adventure. Mary was unable to be with us the entire five weeks, but was scheduled to join us for weeks two and three. Professional friends were perplexed. How could we begin rehearsals without the finished play? An initial draft seemed essential. When I read the first twenty pages of *Windshook* , however, I was confident that Mary Gallagher was onto an exciting piece of theater. My discussions with her only reassured me that this journey would be full and worth the time taken. A large part of this program includes allowing the playwright room to explore without the confines and pressures of commercial success looming over our heads. We had to trust and learn from the writing process. We had to encourage the newcomer and the professional equally if this program was to be worthwhile for everyone involved. I really never feared that Mary would not complete the play within our timeline.

We worked the first week exploring the characters and the world of the play. Since the early pages promised a mysterious resolution, we had a wonderful time suggesting possible outcomes-- first to each other, later to Mary. There was much to do, even with twenty pages. When Mary arrived in San Francisco, she brought another twenty pages with her. We knew more about the story and these people but still didn't know the outcome. Mary said she didn't either. Her creative method was to allow the play to evolve. She attended rehearsals, listened to our ideas, changed some of the first forty pages as we went along and offered insights into the themes and characters. She completed the play the day before she departed. I'll never forget the moment the ending arrived. The energy in the rehearsal studio was electric as we turned the pages, reading for the first time the fate of these people. I've never seen such attention and such wide eyes among teenagers. The final pages of *Windshook*, as you will soon see, are arresting. Like Timothy Mason, Mary Gallagher had answered the challenge set before her with talent, ability, and passion, and given birth to a new and exciting play. Additionally, like Tim, she had touched our lives and offered us a chance to grow as artists. Our audiences, now enthusiastic about this journey, were overwhelmed with what they experienced.

If Timothy Mason and Mary Gallagher were eager to embrace this challenge, Joe Pintauro (our third commission) was hesitant He was unsure if he wanted to grapple with this point of view. He said, "My plays are so far away from anything children are even allowed to see!" It was true that Joe's plays embrace adult issues and that his style is bold and provocative. The same, however, had been true of Mason and Gallagher. I was not expecting thematic equals to Joe's other work, but was more taken by his poetic style, his keen eye for the fantastic and the theatrical, his humanity, and his unique voice. These were all elements I look for when commissioning plays. Timothy and Mary had brought their professional eye and ear to the world of youthful experience with grand artistry and craftsmanship. I felt certain that Joe Pintauro had something very exciting to say in this venue. I'm so glad his spirit of adventure, and his love of young people, won out over his early feelings. *Reindeer Soup* mixes together the essence of Joe Pintauro's other work and goes the extra step of being viewed through young eyes.

Another important telephone call started the wheels of this project turning. After initial discussions about the ideas, possible dates, and the nature of this program, I got a call from Joe while I was visiting my family in Michigan. It was Christmas, 1991. Joe was vacationing in Florida. He called from a pay phone because the telephone in the apartment he was staying in was out of service. We talked for almost an hour about an idea that Joe described as "weird and beautiful." It concerned a family who is on the edge, starving, motherless, with a dysfunctional father. Circumstances lead them north, far up into a frozen tundra, in a desperate attempt to rescue the father's failed life in Detroit. It included an almost holy scene with a dead reindeer (killed by the father) lying on the kitchen table and a mystic, fantastic, eskimo offering hope to them all. So far he had written only a speech given by the eskimo telling the family that in order to survive it was important to eat the dead reindeer, who had been her companion; that reindeer imprinted on humans and sacrificed themselves, when necessary, for us. Joe Pintauro is as passionate a talker as he is a writer and I was in love with the idea. I said, "Please, please, write that play and bring it to San Francisco this summer!"

Like Mary Gallagher, Joe Pintauro could stay only two weeks of the five - week workshop. He was deep into the first production of another play when we began rehearsals. We talked a good deal by telephone before he arrived in San Francisco, making changes here and there helping find clarity that aided the forward movement of our rehearsals. Joe had given us a completed first draft, but promised that things would change. Things did indeed change. We did no less that five full drafts of the play before it was completed. The ending changed two nights before we opened, through a telephone conversation with Joe, who was now back in New York. We all know change is difficult. Change is also very exciting. This is a gifted playwright and the process was thrilling for all of us. The young actors were quite amazing in their ability to absorb the changes, while still moving forward with their characterizations.

Sightings and *High Tide* came to me as gifts from my brother, an actor and writer in Hollywood. He was intrigued with the work we were doing and wanted to contribute--he wanted to challenge himself. If he came up with anything he'd "send it along." *Sightings* came first, almost a year before *High Tide*. This charming and frank exploration of friendship and integrity, beliefs that were tested, and truth, offered us a one-act play for the first time. We worked on Sightings over a five month period before putting it together with *High Tide*. Brad felt passionate about how young people suffer from social ridicule. Julie and Jarred in *Sightings* find truth and a new direction in their lives by testing their beliefs and their friendship in the face of such ridicule. In *High Tide*, young people confront death in a unique, chilling, and often funny afternoon at a Southern California beach. It represents a bold and unsentimental quest for answers. In both plays, I could see the experience of youth with a very personal but universal perspective. Some of the voices here were from my own past. As a young man, Brad, like Brian and Keith in *High Tide*, struggled to reconcile his feelings after the death of a friend. What seemed most moving was how personally the young actors responded to the characters and their words. Brad had spoken the way they felt.

Each of these plays represents a distinctive voice. Each playwright believes in a truth that feels ageless when I read these plays and when I remember the experience of rehearsals and performances. There is a genuine excitement surrounding this body of work. Clearly, we wish to continue. We must keep asking seasoned playwrights to look at the experience of growing up and seek the truth, told with beauty. As young actors and people who wish to help young actors realize their potential, we must continue the respectful joining of hands with these playwrights to gain a stronger technique to our playmaking. We have found that when we unselfishly come together in the name of the theater, in the name of ideas and language, and in the name of growing up, we have the honor to fly a bit higher than before. This infuses our work and our lives and consequently the lives of those we touch by the very nature of this art.

In this volume, you will hear from the playwrights, but you will also hear from some of the young actors who took this journey. Those who were with us for *Ascension Day* were the pioneers. Timothy Mason will forever be in my debt for being the first to say "yes." I applaud all the playwrights and the actors for their courage and their contribution. Many of those actors have continued their theater journey, attending advanced theater programs around the country. Behind them come others. Sara Waldhorn, age nine, was a remarkable *Chrissie* in *Reindeer Soup*. Having experienced this excitement and this process at such a young age can only mean that she will contribute so much more in each future theater venture. That's worth a great deal, don't you think?

I sincerely hope that these plays interest you enough to want to explore them more fully by producing them. Each play provides a rich and lasting promise. I know that as you turn these pages, you will catch the excitement we felt when we first uttered these words.

September, 1992
San Francisco

NEW PLAYS
FROM A.C.T.'S
YOUNG CONSERVATORY

ASCENSION DAY

by Timothy Mason

ABOUT THE PLAYWRIGHT

Timothy Mason has spent most of his life working in theater, first as an actor, and then as a playwright. He has won the National Society of Arts and Letters Award, a playwrighting fellowship from the National Endowment for the Arts, the Hollywood *Drama-Loque* Critics Award for Outstanding Achievement in Theater, the Twin Cities Drama Critics Circle Award, and the Kennedy Center Fund for New American Plays Award.

His plays include *In a Northern Landscape*, first produced by the Actors Theatre of Louisville in 1983; *Levitation*, which premiered in New York City at the Circle Repertory Company in 1984; *Bearclaw*, initially presented in 1984 by Lucille Lortel and Circle Rep at the White Barn Theatre in Westport, Connecticut; *Before I Got My Eye Put Out*, produced in 1985 by the South Coast Repertory in Costa Mesa, California; *Only You*, presented by New York's Circle Repertory in 1987, and *Babylon Gardens*, presented by American Conservatory Theater in San Francisco, and New York's Circle Repertory Company in 1991. Other plays include *The Fiery Furnace*, a new musical for young audiences, *Mr. Popper's Penguins*, and a new screenplay, *Irish Eyes*.

Mr. Mason is a member of the Dramatists Guild and Actors' Equity Association. Manhattan has been his home for the past twelve years, and New York's Circle Repertory, where he is a Company Playwright, has been his theatrical home since 1983.

Ascension Day was commissioned and first presented by the Young Conservatory at the American Conservatory Theater (Edward Hastings, Artistic Director; John Sullivan, Managing Director), San Francisco, California, in August, 1990. It was directed by Craig Slaight; musical direction was by Maureen McKibben; and the assistant to the director was Svetlana Litvinenko.

The cast was as follows:

RANDY .... Kris LeFan
CHARITY........................... Sarita Rodriguez
FAITH................................ Rachel Botchan
JERRY..................................... Andrew Irons
DANNY................................. Joshua Costello
WESLEY .... Nicholas Shenkin
JUNE .... Melissa Stewart-Kern
JOYCE............................ ....Andrea Whitaker
MARY-LOIS............................. Lindsey Hayes

ABOUT THE PLAY

It's a happy surprise when fictional characters display distinctly non-fictional behavior: when they suddenly assert themselves as having lives which precede and follow the raising and lowering of a theatrical curtain. It's as though there were a characters' Bill of Rights, and it's not to be abridged arbitrarily by playwrights.

I experienced this phenomenon forcibly when Craig Slaight commissioned me to write a new play for A.C.T.'s Young Conservatory. There were no strings attached; no suggestions as to theme or subject matter, only the suggestion that the piece address in some way the perspective of the young.

Suddenly three characters from a play I had already written (*The Fierry Furnace*) were clamoring to be heard from again. They didn't come from nowhere, these characters were saying, they each had a history which needed to be told. In *Ascension Day*, I had the great pleasure (and occasional sorrow) of glimpsing them all at another, younger moment in their lives: one which in retrospect would prove to be pivotal.

How do we determine which are the "important" moments in our lives? I think the answer is that we are largely unaware of them. The terrible disappointment which seems at the time barely survivable soon fades into insignificance, while the opening of a

3

minor door may have consequences which last a lifetime.

The teenagers who inhabit the world of *Ascension Day* during this single week in the spring of 1947 are making decisions and discoveries without knowing it: friendships are made and lost, love is revealed or betrayed, relationships are changed, possibly forever. Unaware, these young people are crossing bridges, and each of them by the end of the week is in some way transformed.

Timothy Mason
September, 1992
New York City

CHARACTERS

RANDY, 16
CHARITY, 16
FAITH, Charity's sister, 18
JERRY, 17
DANNY, 16
WESLEY, 17
JUNE, 18
JOYCE, 16
MARY-LOIS, 17

SETTING

The Solid Rock Lutheran Bible Camp, Lake Wissota, Wisconsin, late in May, 1947.

A NOTE TO THE DIRECTOR

Throughout the play, the young characters sing hymns. When this occurs, the notation "SINGERS" is used. It is left to the discretion of the director to decide how many and which of the cast participate in the hymn-singing at different points in the play. In the San Francisco production, the entire cast sang at times; other hymns were sung in quartet, trio, duet and solo.

Ascension Day

Scene 1

Sunday night. We're in the meeting hall of the Solid Rock Lutheran Bible camp located on a Wisconsin lake. It's 1947. The lights are very low, and in the near darkness a group of teenage girls and boys sing.

SINGERS:
Blessed assurance, Jesus is mine!
O what a foretaste of glory divine!
Heir of salvation, purchase of God,
Born of His Spirit, washed in His blood.

This is my story, this is my song,
Praising my Savior all the day long;
This is my story, this is my song,
Praising my Savior all the day long.
(*A single light rises on a 17-year-old boy.*)

RANDY: Hello. Some of you here at camp know me as Randy, some of you don't know me. Most of you don't know me. A few of you know me as Boner. I'm from Stanley, all the friends I have here at Solid Rock Lutheran are from Stanley, that's northeast of Eau Claire and west of Wausau and way northwest of Madison, and anyway we're from Our Savior's over in Stanley and we're glad to be here. For some of you, this is your first time here, this is my second time, I guess nobody here has been here more than twice since this is only the second year that camp has been open after shutting down during the war, but now Japan lies in ruins and we're all glad to be back. Pastor Tollefson asked for testimonies and ... I don't know, nobody else got up, so I guess I'm it. We're going to be doing this for the next week, it'll probably get easier as we go along, but ... It's not always easy to talk about how you stand with Jesus. Kids think you're strange if you do, but most of the kids I know, they already think I'm strange so, you know, I don't have an awful lot to lose. Anyway. I used to have terrible skin. But it says in the Bible, if you have faith the size of a mustard seed, you can move a mountain. And I don't know, but I believe that's just what I did with my acne.

Scene 2

(Sunday night. Charity and Faith are sitting on Faith's bed. Faith is brushing Charity's hair.)

CHARITY: I don't think I could ever do that, how am I ever going to do that?

FAITH: Charity, nobody gets out of here without giving a testimony.

CHARITY: Imagine talking in front of everybody about your complexion problems.

FAITH: Judging from his skin, we're still waiting for the miracle.

CHARITY: Oh, did you think? I thought he was adorable.

FAITH: With you, Charity, this is a broad category.

CHARITY: Strange, but cute as a bug. What was his name? Randy?

FAITH: Oh! Listen. Those loons again ...
(They listen to the wailing of loons across the lake.)

CHARITY: I'm glad you're our junior counselor.

FAITH: So am I.

CHARITY: It's just ... Well, I'm sorry, Faith, but just please try to remember that in some ways it's not easy, having the person in charge of your whole cabin be your sister.

FAITH: You're afraid I'll embarrass you.

CHARITY: Well you know what I mean.

FAITH: Oh, I do. I'll cut back on the chewing tobacco and I'll only spit on the floor after the lights are out.

CHARITY: You get it from Mother, you're so sarcastic, both of you. *(Beat.)* If you could just, you know, be a little more ... I don't know ... Easygoing.

FAITH: What does that mean?

CHARITY: Like, if a boy smiles at you, you don't have to turn to stone or anything.

FAITH: What on earth ... ?

CHARITY: You just don't act like the other girls and that makes them, I don't know ...

FAITH: (*Overlapping.*) I certainly hope I'm not like the other girls...

CHARITY:... uncomfortable.

FAITH:... for one thing, I'm older than the other girls ...

CHARITY: Only a year and a half ...

FAITH:... I'm not a giggling sixteen-year-old.

CHARITY: There, that's just the sort of thing I mean. We're not supposed to giggle or laugh, we're not supposed to goof around or have a good time or ...

FAITH: Charity, of course I want you to have a good time, I don't know what you're talking about. (*Beat*) I want you to have a good time. This is a very special place, this camp meant so much to me last year, I want it to be the same for you, I really do. (*Beat.*) Listen, it's simple. I'll just ask Pastor Tollefson to assign me to another cabin, it doesn't matter to me.

CHARITY: No, Faith, I'm sorry ...

FAITH: Really it doesn't.

CHARITY: No, really.

FAITH: June can take the Naomi cabin, I'll take the Ruth cabin, it's no trouble at all.

CHARITY: No, please ...

FAITH: I think I'd be better with the younger girls anyway.

CHARITY: I wish I hadn't said a thing, I really do.

FAITH: I'm not just saying this ...

CHARITY: Faith, no! Please. I think I'm just nervous, is all, it's the first day, I just want ... you know, people to like me. *(Beat.)* You met somebody here last year, didn't you, that's why it was so special.

FAITH: I met lots of people.

CHARITY: A boy, I mean.

FAITH: And I accepted our Lord as my personal Savior.

CHARITY: Is he here again this year? Wesley? *(Faith stops brushing Charity's hair.)* You wrote his name on the inside back cover of one of your notebooks. About a dozen times. *(The cries of the loons rise again, demented, maniacal.)*

FAITH: There they go again.

CHARITY: They're going crazy out there.

FAITH: It's so mournful, it's so lonely and despairing. *(They listen.)*

CHARITY: *(Finally.)* Can you imagine being that horny?

FAITH: Honest to goodness, Charity, why do you insist on reducing everything to ...

CHARITY: To what?

FAITH: To the lowest common denominator, that's what.

CHARITY: You can't even say it, you can't even say the word.

FAITH: Anyway, you don't know a thing about loons.

CHARITY: And nothing's beautiful to you unless it's mournful and awful and sad and ... touching.

FAITH: They have half a dozen different cries and each one has a different purpose.

CHARITY: I'm just so frightened you'll turn into a spinster.

FAITH: There's one for alarm, there's a feeding call, and yes, of course, there's mating, obviously.

CHARITY: My sister, the spinster Sunday School teacher.

FAITH: There's one particular cry for when they're lost, for when they've become separated and can't find each other. It's a terrible cry, I've heard it, it's so terribly desperate.

CHARITY: Just please ... I need you. I'd be twice as scared if you weren't here.

Scene 3

> (*Sunday night. Jerry, Wesley, Randy and Danny stand on the end of a dock in the lake and look upward. The loons on the lake are even louder out here. Jerry drinks from a pint bottle of brandy.*)

JERRY: (*To the others.*) So you've seen the girls, who do you think'll put out?

RANDY: They've been seeing them all over the country all of a sudden.

DANNY: I read about them somewhere, they call them flying saucers.

WESLEY: And you're saying you saw one here, last year.

RANDY: I did, Wesley, I swear!

Timothy Mason

JERRY: (*To Randy.*) God, you're strange.

RANDY: They're trying to communicate with us, they're trying to make contact.

DANNY: This thing I read said it was the Air Force trying out a new secret weapon to get the Russians. Either that or it was the Russians trying out something new to get us.

JERRY: Am I the only one here interested in a little poon?

WESLEY: The irony would be if it were true, if superintelligent beings actually succeeded in crossing the galaxy, only to make contact with Randy.

JERRY: (*To Wesley.*) God, you ever talk English or do you always use words like that?

RANDY: Some people are saying that when we dropped the atom bomb on the Japs, they could see it out there on the other planets and so they're making contact now because now they know we're a superior species.

JERRY: Great, we don't got one, we got two walking dictionaries.

DANNY: How about that one girl, what's her name?

JERRY: Yeah, I think I know the one you mean, I think you could be right.

DANNY: Va-va-va - voom!

JERRY: There's two of them, they're sisters, and you can just tell, one of 'em's ready to pop. What the hell's her name?

RANDY: If you guys aren't serious about this I think you should go back in the cabin.

DANNY: Sounds good to me, it's cold out here. Jerry, you let Duane catch you with that bottle, Pastor Tollefson's going to barbecue your tail on the end of a weenie fork.

RANDY: They're not going to appear unless you're serious.

JERRY: Yeah, well, you're not gonna get laid unless you get serious. These two got names, it's like they're from the Bible.

DANNY: Oh yeah, I remember, lemme think.

RANDY: There! That light! You see it?

WESLEY: Randy, we see it. It's a cabin, on the other side of the lake.

RANDY: Oh, yeah.

JERRY: Faith!

DANNY: Faith, yeah, that's it. The other one's okay, too, the sister.

JERRY: The other one is second prize. Maybe third or fourth. What I do is I make a list, and then either I cross 'em off or I don't, see what I mean?

WESLEY: You can write?

JERRY: Oh, I bet your teachers just love you. Where're you from?

WESLEY: (*To Randy.*) So, Boner, this thing you saw in the sky, can you describe it?

RANDY: Sure I can, it started as a point of light, like a star, I was standing right here on the end of the dock taking a leak into the lake, and I didn't think a thing about it until it started moving, slow at first and then, golly, it just came at me, and it was getting bigger by the second, and it sort of pulsed, and it went from white to red, and from red to purple and it was getting bigger all the time.

WESLEY: And all this time you were holding your penis in which hand?

RANDY: Hey!

JERRY: (*To Wesley.*) So where're you from, asshole?

Timothy Mason

WESLEY: Uranus.

Scene 4

> (*Low light. The young people sing. At some point during the
> following, Mary-Lois steals a glance at Randy, and Randy
> returns it.*)

SINGERS:
Ye watchers and ye holy ones,
Bright seraphs, cherubim and thrones,
Raise the glad strain,
Alleluia!
Cry out, dominions, princedoms, pow'rs,
Virtues, archangels, angels' choirs,
Alleluia! Alleluia!
Alleluia! Alleluia!
Alleluia!

Scene 5

> (*Tuesday morning. Wesley approaches June.*)

JUNE: Wesley! You're early.

WESLEY: Am I?

JUNE: Welcome to class. Anyway, you're only, what? Two minutes
early. One. You're not even early. Hi.

WESLEY: Hi.

JUNE: So how have you been? I'm fine.

WESLEY: What's this class, I forget.

JUNE: Nature Tips.

WESLEY: Nature Tips.

JUNE: I thought about you, every now and then.

WESLEY: I'm just terrible with names ...

JUNE: June.

WESLEY: June, of course.

JUNE: Wasn't last year great? I thought last year was great. I suppose you've seen Faith.

WESLEY: I've seen her, I haven't had a chance to talk to her.

JUNE: You haven't? You better get busy, Mister. She looks so good.

WESLEY: She always looks good.

JUNE: Oh, I know, I know. I just think she looks ... even better.

WESLEY: She's very good looking.

JUNE: I'm getting married.

WESLEY: Congratulations. Best wishes. Whatever it is you're supposed to say.

JUNE: In the fall. To a soldier. (*Danny enters with Randy.*)

WESLEY: I guess that would have to be the pinnacle of a young girl's dreams.

JUNE: Oh, Wesley, I always loved the way you talk.

DANNY: Oh, Randy, I always loved the way you talk.

RANDY: Go sit on a tack.

JUNE: You children sit down, you're late. I hope you've studied the manual.

DANNY: Children ?

RANDY: She's worse than Duane. (*Joyce enters with Mary-Lois.*)

JOYCE: Hi, June.

MARY-LOIS: Hi, June. Hi, Randy.

JUNE: Have a seat with the others, Wesley. Joyce, I hope I can count on you to lead the class?

JOYCE: I worked on it last night.

DANNY: (*To Randy.*) You can tell just by looking at her, she's memorized the manual.

JUNE: I have just a couple of reminders before we get going. Those of you who are in Nature Tips today will be in Junior Lifesaving tomorrow, and those kids in Junior Lifesaving today will be in Nature Tips tomorrow. Junior Counselors Duane and Faith will be leading the classes for the Little Lambs, and Kenny and I are taking the classes for the Pilgrims of Progress. With Faith assisting me when she can, and me assisting her when I can. Just so you'll know who your group leaders will be. (*Danny snores, Randy enjoys the performance.*) That's adorable, Danny. And it just got you two more demerits. (*Danny "wakes up."*)

DANNY: What? Who? Where am I?

JUNE: Joyce has written an essay for today's class and I'd like to ask her to share it with us now, while I go check on the Little Lambs. Joyce? (*Joyce stands, unfolds a sheet of paper*)

JOYCE: The title of my essay is "Nature: Friend or Foe?"

DANNY: (*To Randy.*) I'm having the most terrible nightmare.

JOYCE: June?

JUNE: Just keep it up, Danny.

JOYCE: "Nature can be a wonderful thing. But there are some things in nature we have to be careful of, especially here at camp." (*June leaves.*) "Some of the things you have to be careful of are chiggers, wasps, deer flies, horse flies and ticks. Before you go to bed each night, be sure you check your body for chiggers and ticks."

DANNY: Hey, Joyce, I'll check you for chiggers if you check me for ticks.

JOYCE: I'm telling June.

DANNY: Great, we can all check each other.

MARY-LOIS: Hey, come on, kids ... (*Wesley leaves.*)

JOYCE: "Skunks carry rabies and so do raccoons: avoid them. Rain is God's gift to us, but if you are out in a boat you could be killed by lightning. Go to shore at the first sign of lightning. When you see three leaves, leave it alone: it could be poison ivy." (*Danny motions to Randy, the two of them rise.*)

MARY-LOIS: (*Fierce whisper.*) Randy! (*Randy shrugs apologetically, and follows Danny out.*)

JOYCE: "The three main poisonous plants are poison ivy, poison oak and poison sumac. Avoid them. As we sing in the hymn, 'This is my Father's world, I rest me in the thought,' but never forget it's also a very dangerous place." Thank you.

MARY-LOIS: Excellent. That was excellent.

Scene 6

    (*Wednesday evening.*)

SINGERS:
This is my Father's world,
And to my listening ears
All nature sings, and round me rings
The music of the spheres.
This is my Father's world,
I rest me in the thought
Of rocks and trees, of skies and seas,

His hand the wonders wrought.

(*A single light rises on Mary-Lois.*)

MARY-LOIS: Hi, I'm Mary-Lois Becker and I'm from Spooner. Tomorrow is Ascension Thursday, the day Our Lord left us to go up to heaven, and Sunday we get on the busses and go home. If this year's anything like last year, a lot of us aren't going to want to get on that bus. Oh, sure, it'll be good to see our folks again ...

JERRY: No, it won't.

MARY-LOIS:... it'll be good to see our folks again and to sleep in a bed that's not filled with sand, a real bed, not an old army cot. And I for one am not going to miss the mosquitoes one little bit. But you know what I mean ...

JERRY: No, we don't.

MARY-LOIS: What I mean is, with the exception of certain individuals, we're already making new friends, and getting closer to old friends, and by the end of the week it's just going to be terribly hard to say goodbye.

JERRY: Hey Mary-Lois, it's hard already!

WESLEY: Hey, Jerry, why don't you shut up?

JUNE: Yeah, Jerry, why don't you shut up. Pastor gave us this time on our own for a reason.

JOYCE: Yeah, Jerry.

MARY-LOIS: Hey, come on, kids ...

RANDY: Yeah, Jerry, why don't you shut up.

DANNY: Yeah, Jerry.

MARY-LOIS: Kids, come on, this is supposed to be a time of devotion ... (*Jerry stands, a little unsteadily.*)

JERRY: Bunch 'a creeps. (*Jerry slowly exits. As he does so, some of the kids applaud.*)

MARY-LOIS: (*After a long unhappy pause.*) To say goodbye to our friends at the end of this week is going to be terribly hard. The friends you make at camp, by the side of a lake, it's different somehow than ordinary life. The smells are different, there's the smell of the pine forest, and the watery smells of the lake, the reeds, the water plants, campfire smoke. Melted marshmallows and chocolate. (*Some scattered cheers for this.*) A skunk in the woods. (*Scattered boos.*) The sounds are different, too. There's the water lapping against the shore, of course. There are the loons. The junior counselors blowing their whistles. (*A mix of cheers and boos.*) And for the rest of your life, I just have this feeling, for me anyway, that the smell of wood smoke is always going to make me think of some of you. I'll see you. I'll hear a loon or bite into a piece of chocolate and I'll see you. Just as you are now. Never any older. Forever. Anyway, Jesus made his friends at the side of a lake, too. For Him, and for them, there was the sound of the water lapping on the shore. The smell of a campfire, of fish cooking on the coals. I'm sure he was happy to go home to see His Father. But think how hard it must have been for Him to leave, too, how terribly hard. And then try to imagine how it must have been for them who were left behind. They had three years with the best Person they'd ever known, Someone who had changed their whole lives forever, and now, suddenly they were alone with the sound of the water on the shore. And everywhere they looked or smelled or listened, there were all these reminders of what they didn't have anymore. Let us pray.

Scene 7

> (*Wednesday night. Outside, Jerry and Charity sit on a bench. It is quite dark. Jerry offers a brandy bottle to Charity.*)

CHARITY: Oh. No. (*Jerry drinks from the bottle.*) It wasn't nice. The way they treated you tonight. (*Jerry finishes the bottle. He's about to throw the empty bottle into the woods when Charity interrupts.*) Don't. Somebody might find it and ... I don't know what they'd do, send you home, call your parents, it'd be awful.

JERRY: The hell do I care?

CHARITY: Here. I'll put it in my purse. A bunch of us are going into town in the morning, I'll drop it in a garbage can. (*Jerry looks at her incredulously.*) No, I mean it. (*Jerry gives her the bottle and she puts it in her purse.*) Your name is Jerry? I mean, I heard the others ... You know, calling you Jerry. Hi.

JERRY: Your sister's name is Faith, right?

CHARITY: Yes.

JERRY: How old is she?

CHARITY: My name is Charity.

JERRY: Right, I knew that. (*Pause*) That's a nice name.

CHARITY: Oh, I just hate it.

JERRY: Yeah, I suppose you could. (*Pause.*)

CHARITY: Where do you live?

JERRY: Chippewa Falls.

CHARITY: No, really, where are you from?

JERRY: I just told you.

CHARITY: You're kidding me. I don't believe it.

JERRY: Why would I joke about a thing like that, I hate it.

CHARITY: I don't believe it, I just ... That's where I live!

JERRY: Oh, yeah? Well, we just moved there.

CHARITY: That's wonderful!

JERRY: It's the crummiest little hole I ever saw.

CHARITY: Well, yes, I guess it's not the greatest little ... Where were you living before?

JERRY: In the second crummiest hole I ever saw.

CHARITY: Well. *(Beat.)* Hi, neighbor!

JERRY: Yeah, right. *(Jerry takes a good look at Charity.)* You know, you're really nice.

CHARITY: I suppose I ought to be getting back to the dining hall.

JERRY: I mean it. The others, they're so damned stuck up.

CHARITY: Well, you know, sometimes people just don't understand other people.

JERRY: What is it about me everybody hates so much?

CHARITY: People don't hate you, Jerry.

JERRY: Yeah? Tell it to the Marines.

CHARITY: Why don't we just go on into the dining hall for some hot chocolate?

JERRY: My old man was killed in Saipan.

CHARITY: Oh, I am just so sorry.

JERRY: He was a hero, he got six Japs before they got him.

CHARITY: You must be so proud.

JERRY: He couldn't stand me.

CHARITY: Oh, I don't believe that for a minute.

JERRY: Yeah, well, maybe not, but he sure got a kick out 'a beating the shit out 'a me.

CHARITY: Oh, Jerry ...

JERRY: The guy my mom's married to now, he pretty much leaves me alone.

CHARITY: Well thank goodness for that at least.

JERRY: He knows I'd kill him. Let's go for a walk.

CHARITY: It's so late, I really think we should just go on into the dining hall.

JERRY: I'm not going back in there.

CHARITY: Jerry, sooner or later you're going to have to.

JERRY: Don't you want to be with me?

CHARITY: Sure I do, Jerry. Let's go on in together.

JERRY: I thought you were different, I really thought you liked me.

CHARITY: I do. I just think ...

JERRY: So come on.

CHARITY: I don't know ...

JERRY: Just a little walk. Down to the dock and back.

CHARITY: Well...

JERRY: Please?

Scene 8

> (*Wednesday night Faith, June, Mary-Lois and Joyce sit and stand on a flight of steps behind the dining hall, drinking hot chocolate. Over the lake, there's a moon.*)

JOYCE: On a night like tonight I can't imagine a thing wrong with the world.

FAITH: You should get a better imagination.

JUNE: Faith, she's fine, stop worrying.

FAITH: It's ten-thirty.

MARY-LOIS: Gosh, I had no idea.

JOYCE: When do you suppose the moon'll be full? It's pretty close.

FAITH: Full moon, June the first—first quarter, June the ninth—new moon, sixteenth of the month.

JOYCE: How do you keep track of things like that?

FAITH: I pay attention. If I hadn't promised her I wouldn't act like her sister while we're here, I'd kill her..

JUNE: When are you going to talk to Wesley?

FAITH: June, just don't.

MARY-LOIS: (*To Joyce.*) Are you going with us into town in the morning?

JOYCE: No, I've got Junior Lifesaving. It's strange, when you're out here it's as though things like towns don't exist, the rest of the world doesn't exist.

MARY-LOIS: Oh, I know.

FAITH: It's been nearly a week, if he wants to talk to me he can come up and talk to me.

JUNE: Not when you've got a look like that on your face.

FAITH: A look like what?

JUNE: I don't know. Mount Rushmore.

FAITH: I am sick to death of people telling me I turn to stone, I

22

don't turn to stone, I am not made of stone, I am made of all the ordinary things people are made of. *(Beat.)*

JUNE: Pardon me. *(Long uncomfortable pause, which Joyce tries to cover with a song, unsuccessfully.)*

JOYCE: *(Singing.)* "By the light of the silvery moon, I want to spoon ..." *(She trails off. Long pause.)*

FAITH: *(To June)* What are you doing in the fall?

JUNE: Oh, it's going to be crazy. George gets demobilized at the end of August, we figure he'll be back home by the first week of September, just in time to help finish getting the crops in. Mom's already working on the dress, and I'll start sending out the invitations and working on the bridesmaids' dresses and turning Dad's den into a home for George and me and that's going to be no picnic, believe me, I think Dad wishes he'd never said okay, he's really going to miss that den. You're going to like your dress, I think, at least I hope, just a very pale purple taffeta with a delicate white lace. The groom's dinner'll be at Weston's Steak House and the rehearsal dinner'll be at the hotel, and we're renting the American Legion club for the reception, and by the thirty-first of October I'll be Mrs. George Nyquist.

FAITH: Oh, yeah, I forgot. *(Beat.)*

JUNE: Faith, you just say things like that to annoy people, you didn't forget my wedding for goodness sake.

JOYCE: *(To June)* Gosh, I envy you.

JUNE: *(To Faith.)* What are you doing this fall?

FAITH: I don't know. Dad'll hire me at the feed-store, I guess.

JOYCE: Marrying a soldier.

JUNE: What about college? Out of our whole class, you were going to be the one who went to college.

FAITH: Out of our whole class, you mean all nine of us? Yeah, I

guess I thought so, too. Chippewa County Community College.
Maybe I still will. Dad doesn't see the point of it. At first I was
upset, but now I'm not sure I can see any point either.

MARY-LOIS: I can't help it, I want to start having babies. As long
as I can remember I've just wanted a baby, a whole lot of babies,
I love babies.

FAITH: Did you ever wonder, if we didn't happen to be born here,
if we were born somewhere else, everything would be different?

MARY-LOIS: What do you mean?

FAITH: I don't know. (*Pause.*)

JOYCE: What is it about a moon that makes you want to be with
someone so bad?

MARY-LOIS: I asked my Aunt Elinor, she's a spinster, I asked her
if she ever missed having children, gosh, I could have bit my lip.
She said, No, I've got my nieces and my nephews, and then she
went upstairs to bed with a migraine headache for the rest of the day.

JOYCE: When I said the moon made me want to be with someone,
I wasn't talking about children.

JUNE: Joyce, we know what you were talking about.

JOYCE: Or your Aunt Elinor.
(*The girls laugh a little. Long pause. Singing.*)
"By the light of the silvery moon,
I want to spoon ..."

JOYCE and MARY-LOIS:
"... To my honey I'll croon love's tune,
Honeymoon keep a-shining in June,
Your silv'ry beams will bring loves dreams
We'll be cuddling soon,
By the silvery moon."
(*Silence. Then it's broken by the sound of someone clapping.*)

JOYCE: Oh, my gosh.

JUNE: Who's there! (*Wesley walks from the shadows up to the steps.*)

WESLEY: That was very nice.

MARY-LOIS: Well it wasn't very nice to scare us half to death.

JOYCE: I can hardly breathe, I've never been so scared in all my life.

JUNE: Come on, girls, time for bed.

JOYCE: Oh, do we have to?

JUNE: I had a hard enough time getting the little girls to bed, now I don't want to hear a peep out of you. (*Joyce and Mary-Lois get up and start out, followed by June.*)

JOYCE: We're going, we're going.

MARY-LOIS: Goodnight.

JOYCE: Goodnight, Faith. Goodnight, Wesley.

FAITH: No, I'm going in, too.

JUNE: (*Like a dart.*) Faith. (*They exit, leaving Faith and Wesley alone.*)

FAITH: How long were you out there?

WESLEY: What is it about a moon, you lose all track of time?

FAITH: You're not funny, you may think you're funny but you're not.

WESLEY: I'm sorry. It's good to see you.

FAITH: Since when? You've been seeing me all week.

WESLEY: You're not the only one who's a little shy.

FAITH: Wesley, you are not shy. I am not shy. We are not shy.

WESLEY: May I sit down?

FAITH: You can stand on your head for all I care. (*Wesley sits.*)

WESLEY: It is pretty, the moon.

FAITH: Okay, I'm turning in. (*Faith stands.*)

WESLEY: Please. Don't. I'm sorry.

FAITH: Thanks for all the letters.

WESLEY: I didn't have anything to say.

FAITH: Goodnight.

WESLEY: Okay, that's not true, I just didn't know what to say.

FAITH: This would be precedent-setting.

WESLEY: Please sit down. (*Faith stands for a long moment looking out into the night.*)

FAITH: Whatever happened to you? You just disappeared.

WESLEY: I know.

FAITH: Oh, Wesley, why did you have to go and ruin everything?

WESLEY: Did I?

FAITH: I think so.

WESLEY: Forever?

FAITH: I don't know. (*Pause.*)

WESLEY: Let's go. Let's just the two of us go.

FAITH: What?

Timothy Mason

WESLEY: I've got my brother's car here. We could be packed up and out of here in an hour.

FAITH: Wait a minute, what are you talking about?

WESLEY: Half an hour. I'm ready to blow up and so are you, I can see it, we're just the same, that's why we found each other last year. If we don't get out of here, we'll die, we'll start screaming or laughing and we won't be able to stop.

FAITH: Hold on, Wesley, just calm down. What on earth is wrong?

WESLEY: You know what's wrong, you were just saying what's wrong, what's wrong is where we were born and if we don't get out now it's going to kill us.

FAITH: I think you must not be feeling well.

WESLEY: No, I'm not feeling well, I can't feel at all in this place, with these people, and neither can you. What's wrong? You going to work for your father in a feed-store, that's what. Jesus, that poor girl so excited she can hardly stand it because she gets to marry some farm boy she's known all her life and move into her father's basement? And the others, they envy her, they actually do! Babies, all I want to do is have babies, lots and lots of babies for the rest of my miserable life, it's pathetic, it's horrifying. And Pastor Tollefson with his wretched testimonies, How I Found God and Got Rid of Pimples, Faith, I just can't take it any more and neither can you. Why should we? We don't have to, where is it written that because we were born in a trap we can't ever get out of it? Where?

FAITH: So what are you proposing, exactly?

WESLEY: Chicago. Chicago.

FAITH: Wesley, that's a city, not a proposal.

WESLEY: We get in my brother's car and go, you and me, we could be in Chicago by morning, we could see the dawn coming over Lake Michigan.

FAITH: And then what?

WESLEY: I don't know exactly. We sell my brother's car, we get a place to stay, we get jobs. We go to the University.

FAITH: The University of Chicago?

WESLEY: Of course. With your mind? Why not? We were born here, Faith, we sure as hell don't have to stay here. (*Pause.*)

FAITH: This is crazy. Why now?

WESLEY: Someone throws a rope to the man who's sinking in quicksand, he says, "Not now, I'm busy sinking." (*Pause.*)

FAITH: What about Charity?

WESLEY: Charity's not like you, you told me that, Charity will be fine here.

FAITH: What about my parents?

WESLEY: You've got all these people in your life saying "I need you, I depend on you, I need you, I need you," and it's not even true, you're just handy, if you weren't here for them to use, they'd just use someone else.

FAITH: You didn't even write.

WESLEY: I'm writing you now. Faith, Come with me, Yours, Wesley. (*Beat.*)

FAITH: You're crazy.

WESLEY: You know, you do look a little like a figure on Rushmore.

FAITH: You are deeply terrible.

WESLEY: Jefferson, I think. (*Wesley kisses her, she is awkward and wishes she weren't. He tries to kiss her again and she breaks away.*)

FAITH: Don't.

Timothy Mason

WESLEY: Why not?

FAITH: For starters, I'm not particularly good at it.

WESLEY: Well, there's only one way to learn.

FAITH: You didn't. Last year. You didn't even try.

WESLEY: When I think how young I was, it's embarrassing.

FAITH: But now, having spent the past year in a bordello near Wausau you're so much older. *(Beat.)*

WESLEY: You're crazy if you think you can stay here with these people and survive.

FAITH: Not a letter, not a postcard, not a word in ten months and you're asking me to marry you?

WESLEY: I'm not asking you to marry me. I'm asking you to live with me.

FAITH: In sin?

WESLEY: In Chicago. *(Long pause.)*

FAITH: I'll think about it. *(Faith begins to leave.)*

WESLEY: Soon. Faith?

FAITH: Not tonight.

WESLEY: Soon. *(She is gone.)*

Scene 9

(The young people sing.)

SINGERS:
Abide with me!
Fast falls the eventide;
The darkness deepens;
Lord, with me abide.
When other helpers
Fail and comforts flee,
Help of the helpless, oh,
Abide with me!

Scene 10

(Thursday morning in the Naomi cabin. Charity and Faith sit on Faith's bed, and Charity brushes Faith's hair. Both girls are far away and very much apart.)

CHARITY: This is going to have to be quick, the bus leaves for town in a few minutes.

FAITH: Yes.

CHARITY: What a great morning.

FAITH: Yes. Have a good time in town.

CHARITY: I will.

FAITH: Good. What are you going for?

CHARITY: Faith?

FAITH: Oh, of course.

CHARITY: It was your idea.

FAITH: Props for the skit, I'm sorry, I just ...

CHARITY: Honey, are you sure you're awake?

FAITH: I'm awake.

CHARITY: You're just so ... Where were you last night, I fell asleep trying to wait up for you.

FAITH: Oh, you know. Thinking. Anyway, where were you?

CHARITY: In bed, sleeping.

FAITH: No, before.

CHARITY: I took a walk.

FAITH: Well, you were out way too late, I was worried sick about you.

CHARITY: So you took a long walk to think about it? *(Beat.)* It's not like when we were little, you don't need to keep track of me every minute of the day.

FAITH: No. I don't, do I.

CHARITY: You certainly don't. *(Beat.)*

FAITH: You're getting along pretty well with Mom and Dad these days, aren't you.

CHARITY: Yes. I guess so. Why?

FAITH: Good. *(Beat.)* And your grades are getting better, aren't they.

CHARITY: Faith, what is all this? There is no one on earth who knows my grades better than you, you know my grades better than me.

FAITH: Better than I.

CHARITY: Than I.

FAITH: I love you, Charity.

CHARITY: Gosh, you can be strange.

FAITH: Have you met anybody nice?

CHARITY: Maybe. (*Charity stops brushing Faith's hair.*) Okay, you're ready to go out and lick the world.

FAITH: Well I sure don't feel like it, I *feel* like the wreck of the Hesperus. It's Randy, isn't it? And you were right, he *is* kind of adorable.

CHARITY: I've got to go.

FAITH: Charity, do you let him kiss you?

CHARITY: Faith!

FAITH: I'm sorry.

CHARITY: If I don't go now, they'll leave without me. What about you?

FAITH: Oh, I'm not going yet.

CHARITY: No, I mean, have you seen that certain special someone whose name starts with "W?"

FAITH: Charity, the way you put things sometimes, it's enough to make a goat throw up.

Scene 11

> (*Thursday morning. Danny stands, June, Joyce, and Jerry sit.*)

DANNY: The purpose of artificial respiration is to get a person who isn't breathing to breathe again. (*Faith joins them.*)

JUNE: You're late.

FAITH: I know.

JUNE: Have a late night? Anyway, you can be the victim.

DANNY: Breathing can stop for several reasons. Electrocution, heart attack, drowning and death. The goal in artificial respiration is to avoid death in the other person and yourself. In electrocution, DO NOT TOUCH THE VICTIM!

JUNE: Danny, please.

DANNY: It was in capital letters in the book.

JERRY: What a dodo.

JUNE: Never mind, just ...

DANNY: In electrocution, do not touch the victim until you have cut off the electricity to the victim. In heart attacks, I haven't read that chapter yet.

JUNE: Just go on to drowning, Danny. Faith is going to be our victim, do we have a volunteer to demonstrate lifesaving? *(Beat.)* Anyone?

JERRY: Sure.

JUNE: You studied the manual?

JERRY: I know how to do it.

JUNE: Okay, good. Do you two want to stand there, while Danny takes us through the procedures?

DANNY: If the victim is still in the water DO NOT ENTER THE WATER UNLESS YOU HAVE TO!

JOYCE: He's impossible.

JUNE: It's really very simple, Danny, do you want your certificate or not?

DANNY: Okay, okay. If you can stay on shore, or on the dock, or in a boat throw the victim a life-preserver or a rope.

JERRY: Faith, catch! (*Jerry mimes throwing Faith a rope; Faith mimes catching it.*)

FAITH: Thanks.

DANNY: If the victim is close enough, hand them an oar if you have an oar. (*Jerry and Faith mime this action.*)

JUNE: Class, what has Danny forgotten? (*Joyce waves her hand madly. Danny mimics her, waving.*) Joyce?

JOYCE: He didn't send someone to get help.

DANNY: Joyce, go get help, you really need it.

JOYCE: Oh, you are so funny.

FAITH: Are we doing this or not?

DANNY: Okay, okay, first you send someone to get help. Especially if she really needs it. Then, if the victim is close enough, you use a rope or a life-preserver or an oar if you have an oar. Friends, Romans, Countrymen—lend me your oars.

JUNE: Joyce, take over.

DANNY: No, please, I can do it.

JOYCE: If the victim is not within reach of the shore or a boat ...

DANNY: Please?

JERRY: Ah, let the dodo do it.

JOYCE: If the victim is not within reach of ...

JUNE: It's your last chance, Danny.

FAITH: Come on, Danny, it's my last chance, too, I'm drowning.

JOYCE: June, no fair, you said I could.

FAITH: Joyce, you stand in danger of growing up to be a terrible drip.

DANNY: If you have to go in the water to save the victim, always approach the victim from behind.

JUNE: Jerry? (*Jerry takes a position immediately behind Faith.*)

DANNY: Make a crook out of your left arm and put it around the victim's neck.

JOYCE: (*Waving her hand in the air.*) That's if you're righthanded, if you're left-handed you do it with your right arm.

DANNY: Thank you, Miss Two-Shoes.

FAITH: (*To Jerry.*) Okay, go easy.

JERRY: Don't worry, I know how to do this.
(*Jerry puts his left arm around Faith's neck.*) Hey, it's okay.

FAITH: I know, I get tense.

JERRY: It's okay.

DANNY: DO NOT LET THE VICTIM, sorry, do not let the victim control you. If the victim is thrashing too hard ...

JUNE: Class, there's something Danny missed, what is it?

DANNY: Miss Two-Shoes?

JERRY: The talking, you gotta be talking to them all the time, letting them know it's gonna be all right. It's gonna be all right, Faith, don't worry.

FAITH: If you say so.

JERRY: Just relax now, let me carry you.

DANNY: But no! She's thrashing around and pulling you under. Thrash, thrash, pull, pull! JERRY, JUST LET GO!

JERRY: I'm not gonna let go of you, Faith, you just let yourself go limp and I'll carry you home.

JOYCE: But he's supposed to let go and start again if she's thrashing.

FAITH: Joyce, I'm not thrashing, do you see me thrashing? (*Jerry's arm is around Faith's neck, and the two of them walk slowly, Jerry stroking with his right arm as though he were slowly swimming.*)

JERRY: My old man did this for me once.

FAITH: Really?

JERRY: He saved my life.

DANNY: (*Singing.*) "Here comes the bride,
Long, tall and wide ..."

JERRY: Shoot, he'd do anything for me. The Germans got him during the Normandy Invasion.

FAITH: I'm very sorry. (*Pause.*)

JUNE: That's really good, guys. (*Randy runs in.*) Okay, you've got the victim on shore. Now what do you do?

RANDY: Excuse me.

JUNE: Randy, please. Joyce, I want you to take us through artificial respiration.

DANNY: Roger and out.

RANDY: (*To June*) Can I talk to you?

JOYCE: You lay the victim on their belly on the ground and you clear their mouth of vomit and if they've swallowed their tongue you pull it back out and you turn their head to the side.

JUNE: Excellent.

JOYCE: You press down on their back, two, three, you lift up from their elbows, two, three ...

RANDY: Excuse me. Faith, Charity's in trouble.

FAITH: What?

RANDY: In the hardware store, I asked her to lend me forty cents for a flashlight and she opened her purse and Pastor Tollefson saw a brandy bottle in it, there was a bottle of brandy in her purse. He's calling your parents. (*Jerry disengages himself from Faith. The others draw away from her. Charity enters and sits.*)

CHARITY: Please don't look at me like that.

Scene 12

> (*Low lights. The young people sing.*)

SINGERS:
Just as I am, without one plea
But that Thy blood was shed for me
And that Thou bidd'st me come to Thee,
O Lamb of God, I come, I come.

Scene 13

> (*Thursday. Faith and Charity alone. Charity is terrified.*)

CHARITY: Please don't look at me like that.

FAITH: I'm not looking at you, I don't even want to look at you. (*Beat.*) Who did Pastor talk to, Mom or Dad?

CHARITY: Mom first, then Dad.

FAITH: Oh, gee. (*Pause. Loons on the lake.*) Did you talk to them?

CHARITY: Just to Mom, for a minute. Dad wouldn't.

FAITH: How did she sound?

CHARITY: Imagine the worst.

FAITH: Deeply disappointed.

CHARITY: Deeply disappointed.

FAITH: But they're not necessarily coming?

CHARITY: They'll come, I know they will. Dad wouldn't miss a chance like this. And I have to give a testimony that Pastor Tollefson approves of. Pastor Tollefson said he was doing me a favor by not sending me home. I think I'd really rather die.

FAITH: No, you wouldn't. (*Beat.*) Charity, what have you been doing?

CHARITY: I never drank a drop.

FAITH: Then how ... ?

CHARITY: I can't tell you.

FAITH: This affects more than just you, you know, it affects me, I had plans, I had hopes.

CHARITY: What are you talking about? I've never been so humiliated in all my life and I'm about to get killed for something I didn't even do, and all you're thinking about is yourself.

FAITH: Did you get it from Randy?

CHARITY: I can't tell you. Even if I told you, how is that going to help me with Dad or Pastor Tollefson or Mom? "Dad, I didn't drink any, this boy I know drank it all and gave the bottle to me," they'd kill me.

FAITH: How far has it been going? Have you been going all the way with him? *(Beat.)* Charity?

CHARITY: You're eighteen years old, Faith, and for all I know you've never even been kissed. I'm not the abnormal one. *(Beat.)*

FAITH: I'm sick of you. I'm sick of you and these people and Dad and all of it, and I'm not going to wait around for the explosion, I'm getting out of here now.

CHARITY: Well go then! Anyway, where would you go?

FAITH: When I'm not here you'll just use somebody else. *(Charity goes to Jerry, leaving Faith alone.)*

Scene 14

    (Thursday evening. Charity and Jerry.)

JERRY: What are you talking about? What do you want me to do? *(Beat.)* This isn't anything, this is nothing.

CHARITY: You don't know our father.

JERRY: An empty pint of brandy?

CHARITY: You don't know him.

JERRY: Does he hit you?

CHARITY: No.

JERRY: Then what the hell are you so afraid of?

CHARITY: He looks at you.

JERRY: You're crazy. He looks at you? If I tell them the bottle was mine, I get sent home and that asshole beats me bloody, but you are afraid somebody's gonna look at you.

CHARITY: You said he doesn't touch you.

JERRY: Well he does, all right? He does. Shit. I wish I never met you.

CHARITY: Jerry, please, I'm sorry, I didn't know. I'll be all right, really. Just don't say you wish you never met me, you know how much I love you, I showed you how much I love you.

JERRY: Oh, go away. Lemme go!

Scene 15

(*Low light. The young people sing.*)

SINGERS:
Just as I am and waiting not
To rid my soul of one dark blot,
To Thee, whose Blood can cleanse each spot,
O Lamb of God, I come, I come.

Scene 16

(*Thursday night. Randy and Mary-Lois.*)

RANDY: Mary-Lois, please? Come down to the dock with me, they're coming tonight, I know it. It's terrible being the only one who's seen it, I want someone else to see it.

MARY-LOIS: Why me?

RANDY: I don't know. Because you're a believer.

MARY-LOIS: That's a different thing altogether.

RANDY: Because you believe in things you can't see, you believe in things other people don't believe in.

MARY-LOIS: That doesn't mean I believe in ... Randy, I don't even know what you're talking about, what am I supposed to be believing in?

RANDY: I don't know, exactly. Me?

MARY-LOIS: Well that goes without saying.

RANDY: Really? *(Beat.)*

MARY-LOIS: Last year you didn't even look at me.

RANDY: Last year I had terrible skin.

MARY-LOIS: Boy, you don't know a thing about women. *(Beat.)* How do you know they're coming tonight?

RANDY: You'll laugh.

MARY-LOIS: Now that's one thing you know I won't do.

RANDY: They told me. *(Pause.)*

MARY-LOIS: Well, if they told you, we'd better be there to say hello.

RANDY: Gosh. You're great.

MARY-LOIS: You think so?

RANDY: Yes.

MARY-LOIS: Then why for the love of Pete didn't you ever say so?

RANDY: Come on, let's go. *(They leave.)*

MARY-LOIS: How, exactly, did they tell you? Randy?

Scene 17

> *(Thursday night. Faith approaches Wesley.)*

WESLEY: Faith?

FAITH: I'm sorry, did I startle you? I just couldn't wait another minute, I should have knocked.

WESLEY: No, it's fine.

FAITH: By now you'll have heard about the scandal.

WESLEY: What? Oh, your sister, yeah, I'm sorry.

FAITH: It just came to me, how tired I am of all of this, you were right, this isn't for me, I don't belong here, I belong with you and both of us belong somewhere else, a long long way from here.

WESLEY: Faith, just a minute now, calm down. This isn't life or death, is it?

FAITH: No, it's just death. It's not the religion so much, it's how they understand it, which is not at all, they don't get it, there's no room in their puny little hearts to get it and their minds are tiny and I'm just sick of it. You're going to think I'm terrible, but I just realized ... It's hard to say it, even, but I just realized that I don't even like my Dad, he's so hard, it's like he's made of stone, and he's on his way here now with that stone look of his and I know that I could turn out that way, I could turn to stone if I don't get out now. *(Beat.)* I'm sorry, I just ... *(Beat.)* What's that? That's a suitcase. Is that your suitcase? *(Pause. Faith begins to be frightened.)* Great. You're all packed up.

WESLEY: I was going to come by.

FAITH: I'm not packed but I could be. In about one split second. *(Beat.)* Why were you coming by? *(Beat.)* Wesley, did I wait too long?

WESLEY: Last night, I spoke without thinking, I should have thought about it all before I said a thing. *(Beat.)*

Timothy Mason

FAITH: And? *(Beat.)* You've had a chance to think, so now you can talk. Talk.

WESLEY: For one thing, there's my brother's car. I can't just take it, he worked all last summer to get that car, it was a big deal him lending it to me, it wouldn't be right, he was doing me a favor.

FAITH: I see.

WESLEY: So I figure, first I'll go home, I'll see him and we'll talk about it, maybe he can give me a lift, you know?

FAITH: Oh, of course.

WESLEY: And then there'd be my parents to deal with, and borrowing money, and if you were with me, God, the questions, it'd be really uncomfortable for you.

FAITH: Terribly.

WESLEY: I mean, it wasn't fair to you, it wasn't fair to me, we haven't even been going together, and here I was, asking you to pack up and run out on everything and ...

FAITH: And live with you.

WESLEY: Yes, it was crazy. I mean, God, Faith, one kiss?

FAITH: Crazy.

WESLEY: I'm going to be in touch, this time I'll write. *(Beat.)* As soon as I get to Chicago, I'll ...

FAITH: *(Overlapping.)* I'll look forward to that.

WESLEY: Okay.

FAITH: I'll look forward to that. *(Wesley picks up his suitcase and goes.)*

Scene 18

SINGERS:
Our God, our Help in ages past,
Our Hope for years to come.
Our Shelter in the stormy blast,
And our Eternal Home.

Scene 19

> (*Faith sits on a bench. After a few moments, Jerry enters. It is quite dark*)

JERRY: Who is that? Is that you?

FAITH: I have no idea.

JERRY: Faith?

FAITH: Go away, Jerry. I'm not in the mood to talk.

JERRY: Neither am I. (*Pause.*) I need you.

FAITH: Oh, great. Perfect. *(Beat.)*

JERRY: Can I sit here?

FAITH: May I. *(Beat.)*

JERRY: May you what?

FAITH: Sit down, Jerry. (*Jerry sits.*)

JERRY: I'm not feeling too good.

FAITH: Neither is anybody. (*Faith looks at Jerry.*) You're really kind of a mess, aren't you. And still you swagger around here like you're Frank Sinatra.

Timothy Mason

JERRY: Tonight is the third anniversary of my Dad's death. *(Beat.)*

FAITH: You have a father you can be proud of.

JERRY: Goddamn right.

FAITH: Don't swear, I don't like it.

JERRY: Sorry. *(Beat.)* Did I swear?

FAITH: Jerry, would you put your arm around my neck?

JERRY: Sure. *(He does so.)* That was pretty good today, in Junior Lifesaving. *(Beat.)* I saved your life. *(Faith kisses him.)* From the minute I saw you ...

FAITH: Don't say a word.

Scene 20

SINGERS:
A thousand ages in thy sight
Are like an evening gone,
Short as the watch that ends the night
Before the rising sun.

Scene 21

    (Thursday night. Charity alone.)

CHARITY: Faith? Hello? Where is everybody? Faith? *(The loons on the lake are crying wildly.)* Where did everybody go? *(Loons.)* Please?

Scene 22

> (*June, Danny and Joyce on a bank above the lake. Loons crying.*)

JUNE: Here on the banks of Lake Wissota, right here where we're sitting, there was a settlement of Chippewa Indians about a hundred years ago, and this particular tribe was very important in the Chippewa Nation. It was, I don't know, a capitol city or something. Or royalty, the members of this tribe were very high up in the scheme of things.

DANNY: And once upon a time ...

JOYCE: Just listen, will you?

JUNE: And once upon a time, in this tribe, there was a princess.

DANNY: I knew it.

JOYCE: Gosh, you irritate me.

JUNE: That's because he's in love with you, Joyce, learn to recognize the signals. (*Danny briefly puts a finger down his throat and gags.*) Anyway, it's the old story: the princess was supposed to marry the prince of a neighboring tribe, but of course she was already in love with a young hunter of her own tribe. They found them the night before the wedding ceremony was to take place. They were in a canoe out just there, beyond the point, trying to escape, when a fleet of canoes set out from the shore to stop them. The princess told her hunter to go on paddling, while she picked up the hunter's bow and started shooting. The legend says the water was stained red in the moonlight with the blood of the pursuers. But in the end, they overtook the young couple and the princess's father, the great chief of them all, boarded their canoe. It was all over in a moment: the chief's spear in the hunter's heart, and the hunter sinking to the bottom of the lake. Before anyone could do anything, the beautiful princess dove after him, swimming down, down through the dark water, searching for her lover. And she's been searching for him ever since. Sometimes, on a moonlit night, you can see her, glowing red with blood, surfacing like a loon and crying because she can't find him. *(Beat.)* And that's the story of Lake Wissota.

Scene 23

> *(Jerry goes to the bench and sits heavily. He looks around, takes a pack of cigarettes from a pocket and lights one. Faith enters and sits on the bench. Long silence.)*

FAITH: Let me have one of those. *(Jerry flips a cigarette from his pack, stamps it, gives it to Faith and lights it for her. She puffs without inhaling.)* What do you want to do when you ... What are you planning to do when you get out of school?

JERRY: I don't know. You?

FAITH: I'm already out of school, I'll work at my father's feedstore in the fall as a cashier.

JERRY: I worked in a filling station last year.

FAITH: Oh, yeah?

JERRY: Hated it. *(Pause.)*

FAITH: I'll probably move up to accountant after my first year.

JERRY: I might join the army.

FAITH: Your father was in the army?

JERRY: Hell, no.

FAITH: Which branch was he in?

JERRY: Oh, yeah, for a couple of years he was. *(Jerry looks around.)* Boy, it's like the place is deserted. *(Pause.)*

FAITH: I hate it. This cigarette, I hate it. *(She drops it on the *ground and steps on it.)*

JERRY: I got something you might like. *(Jerry takes a pint of brandy from a pocket. He uncaps it and offers it to Faith, who makes no move to touch it, but stares at Jerry.)* Don't you want some?

FAITH: This is what?

JERRY: Four-Stars.

FAITH: And Four-Stars is what?

JERRY: God. Brandy. *(Beat.)*

FAITH: You bastard. You son of a bitch.

JERRY: Hey, what I do? *(Faith stands.)*

FAITH: You bastard. You bastard. *(Faith leaves.)*

Scene 24

> *(Thursday night. Faith goes to Charity's bed and shakes her.)*

FAITH: Charity. Charity.

CHARITY: Stop that, I'm not asleep.

FAITH: I'm so sorry, I'm so sorry for the things I said, Charity, I love you, I get sick of you sometimes, everyone gets sick of everybody sometimes, but I care about you and I worry about you and I'm so terribly sorry.

CHARITY: Okay, okay. *(Beat.)* I love you, too. Where on earth were you? Where was anybody, nobody was anywhere.

FAITH: You've got to stop it with Jerry, he's a terrible person, I don't want you to see him ever again. *(Beat.)*

Timothy Mason

CHARITY: Who told you it was him?

FAITH: He's disgusting, he doesn't care about anyone, and he's the most terrible liar and I hate him with all my heart. *(Beat.)*

CHARITY: Why would you say such awful things? Who's been talking to you?

FAITH: Nobody's been talking to me, I just know. *(Beat.)*

CHARITY: Faith, that is so cheap. I never thought you could be so cheap. To be so jealous, just because I've got a guy and you don't.

FAITH: Oh, for God's sake.

CHARITY: Don't you ever talk to me about Jerry again. Geez, this hurts. I love him, Faith, you may not know what that word means but I do. *(Beat.)*

FAITH: There's nothing I can say, is there.

CHARITY: We've got Dad and Mom coming tomorrow, and I have to have a testimony ready, and I want to hear it from you that you will not tell them about me and Jerry until we're engaged.

FAITH: Engaged.

CHARITY: Nothing, Faith, I don't want a word out of you. It's going to be hard enough as it is.

FAITH: I'm in quicksand. I'm sinking. *(Loons on the lake, wild, frantic, desolate)*

Scene 25

(The young people sing.)

SINGERS:
A thousand ages in Thy sight
Are like an evening gone,
Short as the watch that ends the night
Before the rising sun.
Time, like an ever-rolling stream,
Bears all her sons away ...

Scene 26

(Thursday night. Randy and Mary-Lois on the end of the dock.)

MARY-LOIS: It's so hard to believe.

RANDY: I know.

MARY-LOIS: It's so beautiful.

RANDY: Yes.

MARY-LOIS: It moves so fast.

RANDY: Yes.

MARY-LOIS: I'm a little scared.

RANDY: So am I.

MARY-LOIS: I think it's coming from God.

RANDY: I never thought of that.

MARY-LOIS: But don't you think maybe it could be?

RANDY: Here it comes.

MARY-LOIS: Let's have lots of babies.

RANDY: Wow. Okay. Not yet, okay?

MARY-LOIS: Hold my hand.

RANDY: I'm holding it.

(*Lights out.*)

THE END

WINDSHOOK

by Mary Gallagher

ABOUT THE PLAYWRIGHT

Mary Gallagher's plays *Father Dreams, Little Bird, Chocolate Cake, Buddies, Bedtime, Dog Eat Dog, Love Minus, How To Say Goodbye* and, *¿De Donde?* have been published by Dramatists Play Service and produced by theaters across the country and abroad. A recipient of the Susan Smith Blackburn prize for *How To Say Goodbye* and the Rosenthal New Play Award for *¿De Donde?*, she has been honored with awards from the NEA, the New York Foundation for the Arts, the Rockefeller and Guggenheim foundations, the New Dramatists residency at the Tyrone Guthrie Center in Ireland, and the Office for Advanced Drama Research. Mary Gallagher has published stories and two novels, and with Ara Watson wrote the CBS-TV movie *Nobody's Child*, which was directed by Lee Grant and starred Marlo Thomas, and received the 1986 Writers Guild Award and the Luminas Award from Women in Film. Her plays *Fly Away Home* (later titled *Little Bird*) and *Father Dreams* were developed in A.C.T.'s Plays-in-Progress program in 1977 and 1978, respectively. She recently completed a film for CBS-TV, *Bonds of Love*, with Treat Williams and Kelly McGilliss.

Windshook was commissioned and first presented by the Young Conservatory at the American Conservatory Theater (Edward Hastings, Artistic Director; John Sullivan, Managing Director), San Francisco, California, in August, 1991. It was directed by Craig Slaight; musical direction was by Maureen McKibben; and the assistant to the director was Svetlana Litvinenko.

The cast was as follows:

DARLENE . . . . Tyson Sheedy
MOM . . . . Tyson Sheedy
RUBY . . . . Rainbow Rachel Underhill
DYLAN . . . . Andrew Irons
RAFE . . . . Devon Angus
JULIE . . . . Shona Mitchell
JACKIE . . . . Pavlos Politopoulos
LANCE . . . . Jon Lucchese
DAD . . . . Andrew Irons and
Jon Lucchese
BROOKS . . . . Pavlos Politopoulos

ABOUT THE PLAY

When Craig Slaight approached me about writing a play for the Young Conservatory, I had no idea what I would write about. But I've done some of my best work because I was commissioned by a theatre. That act of faith - "We'll pay you to write any play you want" - is the opposite of the indifference which playwrights feel swamped by most of the time, and it really puts heart into you. It makes you want to write something terrific just to show those people that they were right to have that faith in you.

But I was also nervous. There's so much obvious writing about teenagers. I wanted to write something that would strike a deep chord in the young actors without being a "teenage issue" play. And I didn't want the young actors to play, in a supposedly realistic way, much older characters.

I had had the urge to write a play based on the Child Ballad, "The Mill o' Tifty's Annie, " for six years. After I was commissioned, it struck me that the main characters in the story - the young girl, her lover and her brother - could all be quite young, and the play could be a story acted out for the audience by young people. The same actors who played the young characters could play the adults in primitive masks, taking the curse off the "unrealistic" aspect of this casting, and strengthening the audience's sense of the huge gulf which is a major cause of their destruction. I also felt that I could explore the stupid and random violence of the Persian Gulf war through this story of needless family violence which became random, as all violence does.

So I started writing. But it came very slowly. I had been writing screenplays for a living for several years, a process in which I'd had to figure out the whole plot before I could actually write a single scene. I was determined to get back to organic writing for *Windshook*, to take all the time I needed to let the story flow from inside me without my knowing what would happen next.

Craig Slaight was wonderfully patient and supportive while I was following my nose through the play. Most directors and artistic directors want your play to be finished before they start rehearsals - which is like asking an actor to give his whole performance at his first audition. But when I sent Craig only 20 pages, a month before rehearsals, he responded with tremendous enthusiasm, without pressuring me to hurry. I kept working slowly and organically, and he kept giving me support. As a result, the first draft of *Windshook* was the strongest I've ever written. It didn't have any of the long-winded detours I take when I don't know where I'm going, and have to cut out later.

Once in rehearsal at the Young Conservatory, the fascination and emotional conviction of the young actors reminded me of why I went into the theatre in the first place. Now I have a picture of the YC cast and crew on my bulletin board, to remind me of the one thing that really matters to me in the theater a shared impulse to try to tell the truth.

Mary Gallagher
September, 1992
Kerhonkson, New York

CHARACTERS

RUBY   18. The prettiest girl in town, and the stubbornest.

RAFE   20. Ruby's brother. A romantic who will not be sidetracked, even by himself.

DYLAN   20. The stranger Ruby falls in love with. Drifts where the wind is blowing, till he finds something he wants.

LANCE   20. Ruby's would-be boyfriend and Rafe's friend. A talented dirt-track racer. Volatile, impulsive, and a drinker.

JACKIE   20. Rafe's best friend. Sensitive but practical, a good guy.

DARLENE   17. Ruby's best friend. Married to a loser and mother of a toddler, accepts her lot with humor and deep fatalism.

JULIE   20. Rafe's girlfriend. She can change everything else in her life except her love for Rafe.

Adult Characters Played by Masked Actors

DAD   Early 40s. Rafe and Ruby's dad. Gregarious and funny, but it masks enormous bitterness. Played by same actors as Dylan and Lance.

MOM   Early 40s. His wife. Seems worn out but harbors a secret dream. Played by same actress as Darlene.

BROOKS   Early 30s. The man with money who changes other people's lives without thinking of consequences. Played by same actor as Jackie.

SETTING

The story takes place in a rural area, two hours drive from a large city, during the summer and fall of 1991. Scenes happen in and out of doors in many different places.

Windshook

Lights up on Darlene. She dangles a mask in one hand. To the audience

DARLENE: After it happened, I just couldn't even go over to their house or nothing, not for weeks. I wouldn't even walk past it when I was wheeling Ashley, I'd go around by the back road past the old fire house. It's way out of the way, and we was having heavy rains, that back road was awash, just about...but I just felt so bad...But when I did go see her mom, finally, go by just to see did they need anything or what...her mom said the saddest thing to me. She said, "I was the one who started it all up, Darlene. I seen him on the road, first day he was in town here, and I pointed him out to her. That's where it all begun."

Lights up on Ruby as she enters. She wears jeans and heavy work gloves smeared with dirt. Her hair is raked back carelessly. Darlene puts on the "Mom" mask, is now Ruby's mom.

RUBY: Ma, you want me to spray the tomatoes too?

MOM: Course I do, wadaya think? (*As Ruby turns away, Mom lowers her voice*) Ruby - look at this kid that's passing. (*Dylan, with a backpack and bedroll, enters Downstage, walking slowly along the road, looking around with interest and pleasure at the countryside.*) Don't he look like Dirk, who used to be on my soap?(*Ruby looks. Impressed, but keeping it to herself.*)

RUBY: ...He don't look like much to me.

MOM: Choosy, ain't ya?...You don't know him?

RUBY: No. (*Dylan stops, crouches, dumps his pack and sits.*)

MOM: What's he doing out so far from town...? Oh, look, he's sitting down there by the creek - go on and wander by.

RUBY:(*Laughs.*) Get out!

MOM: Go on! He's cute!

RUBY: He'd know why I was doing it.

MOM: Well, ain't that terrible, for him to know.

RUBY: You go and wander by.

MOM: I'll tell ya, if I was your age, I'd be after him. And I'd git him, too.

RUBY: If he's around, I'll meet him soon enough.

MOM: (*As Ruby exits:*) Must be nice to be so cocky...(*Darlene drops the mask. As herself, to the audience:*)

DARLENE: That's where it all begun.

Crossfade as Darlene and Dylan exit. Rafe enters. He wears a U.S. Army combat helmet, a white T-shirt, jeans and boots, holds a standard-issue Army automatic weapon. He speaks to the audience

RAFE: There just wasn't no work for me. That's how it is around here. You get outa high school, and there's only two places to go - the prison or the army. I like to hunt - learned hunting from my dad. About the only good times we had when I was coming up was out there in the woods in deer season, or shooting wild turkeys or coons. You take and shoot an animal...you do it right, you use the meat to feed your family...there's a meaning, there's a purpose to it. But to make your living keeping other men locked up - I couldn't see my way to spending my whole life like that. Them guards, they got their pensions in their minds first day they walk inside those gates. They're lifers, worse than cons are. I wanted more than that. (*Julie enters, carrying a big yellow bow with trailing ribbons. She stares at Rafe approaches. He looks at her. To Julie*) I wanted more...and I *knew* what I wanted. Since I was a little kid, I always had that dream. But my dad always said, "You can't eat bread you haven't earned." And ain't no way he'd ever go beyond that...not for me. So... (*Julie pins the bow on Rafe's shirt. He holds her gaze, neither of them yielding, as Ruby and Darlene as Mom enter and decorate the stage with big yellow bows and long trailing yellow ribbons. Rafe goes on, to Julie:*) But the army...it didn't work for me. (*To the audience again:*) You make a mistake and three guys rub your nose in it, like you're a dog that shit indoors. And when the

Mary Gallagher

war came...we just sat and sweated. Or drilled and sweated and passed out. Guy in our outfit died in his gas mask and protective suit, got too hot in there and he couldn't get it off and panicked, had a heart attack. We went over in September, and before we even got there, we had packages from strangers waiting, sitting in the desert and waiting for us to come. Boxes full of cookies and candy bars and lollipops, all melted down and beat to shit from sitting in the desert, and the slap-second you opened 'em, they was full of sand. And razor blades and toilet paper, like the Army hadn't thought of stuff like that, and little gift-type stuff, Ninja Turtle key chains and Dick Tracy coffee mugs, whatever else they thought might remind us of home, I guess...*(To Julie:)* And all these letters thanking us and praising us, from strangers...thousands of these letters...all of 'em full of sand.*(Dylan enters, wearing the "Dad" mask - he's Ruby and Rafe's Dad. A worn feed cap is part of the mask. Dad has a six-pack of cheap U.S.-made beer, hands out beers to Lance and Jackie, friends of Rafe who enter with him, and to Mom, Julie and Rafe. Ruby takes Rafe's helmet and gun and exits. This is Rafe's welcome-home party. Rafe speaks to the others now:)* Sand in all the gear, the tanks shut down. Sand in your eyes, your teeth...and we couldn't even drink beer cause the towelheads don't believe in beer. Had our cots in ditches and couldn't keep the rats out, cause anything can crawl through sand. Guys got bit, got sick...sick with these diseases that don't exist no more. But the worst part was just sitting. You go over there all rared up for a fight...and then you got to sit on it...We took it out on each other, some.

DAD: Sure ya did. It's human. Sure.

RAFE: Then come to find out, it was over, and we won. Coming home as heroes, and we hadn't done nothing.

LANCE: But you were *in* it! And we kicked their ass!

RAFE: I didn't.

DAD: Well, I don't guess I know as much as Rafe here about such things, but I'll just say one thing and then I'll shut up. When we was in Viet Nam, we knew why we was there and we knew what to do about it.

RAFE:*(Beat; then:)* I'm not saying I had any problem about it.

DAD: Oh good, well, that eases my mind. Where's that girl got to? (*Dad drinks his beer as Ruby enters with an open fifth of whiskey and a shot glass, comes to Dad:*)

MOM:(*To Rafe:*) D'you see all them little yellow bows along the fence? Julie and me did all that, day after you left. Took the best part of the afternoon.

RAFE: Looks nice, Mom.

DAD:(*Hits Ruby on the butt.*) Just pour that out for your old man. (*Ruby pours the shot and Dad takes it as Mom says to Rafe:*)

MOM: Julie come around to see me quite a bit while you was gone. She helped me out more than your sister. With the garden and the farmstand too.

DAD:(*Holding up the shot glass.*) Here's hoping all you good people live forever and I sit right beside you.(*They all drink. Dad sits, slaps his knee.*) Come on, Rube, sit with your old man once before you git too big.

RUBY: (*Sits on Dad's lap.*) I'm too big already.

DAD: Oh, you ain't too big to spank.

LANCE: I'll spank her for you. (*Ruby ignores this, withering him.*)

DAD: I wouldn't put money on ya. (*Laughs, slaps Lance's back. To Ruby:*) Don't be so stingy with that bottle, Rube. (*As Ruby pours a shot and Dad gives it to Lance.*)

JACKIE: (*To Rafe:*) We gotta get up to the Windshook Creek and catch some trout, now you're home. I been cleaning house up there. Only good fishing spot them city people ain't found yet.

LANCE: Hey, you want to go hunting Sunday, shoot a couple turkeys? Easier than shooting them sand-niggers, huh?

RAFE: I didn't shoot nobody, I told ya.

DAD: Jackie, come on over here and have a real drink. (*Jackie goes* *to Dad. Ruby pours him a shot.*)

JULIE: (*To Rafe, privately:*) My stepdad says they need people up to the prison. And you wouldn't have to work a cellblock, you could work the sawmill crew, maybe, or on the farm, if my stepdad spoke for you.

RAFE: That's still the prison. Ain't no different.

JULIE:...Well...(*Shrugs.*)...what *are* you gonna do?

DAD: (*As Jackie drinks:*) How's that now, is that smooth? (*Jackie nods.*) Attaboy.

JULIE: (*To Rafe:*) You know, I did write you a letter.

RAFE: I got *one.*

JULIE: Well, I got *one* from you. (*They look at each other, then away, neither backing down.*)

RUBY:(*Takes the shot glass from Jackie.*) My turn.

DAD: Listen to this, now...You will, will ya?

RUBY: Can I?

DAD: (*Proud of her.*) Aw hell, just don't say who give it to you. (*She holds the glass as Dad pours. Mom, alone and feeling the old wound of her exclusion, watches. Rafe is also aware of being excluded, but won't look at them.*)

RAFE: (*To Julie:*) What you been doing since I left?

JULIE: (*Letting him wonder.*)...Not too much.

RAFE: How much is too much? (*Julie has to smile. Rafe smiles too contact.*)

DAD: Watch this here, now. (*Rafe and Julie also look as Ruby drains the shot, seemingly nonchalant. Dad, Lance and Jackie laugh.*) Now where d'you think she gets that from?

MOM: (*Blurts:*) Marlin, she's too young for that.

DAD: Yes, dear. (*To Lance and Jackie:*) My Uncle Percy always told me, "Only two words a married man's got to know - 'Yes, dear.' You learn how to say them words and you'll be all right."

RAFE: Uncle Percy had three wives. Kept leaving 'em. Has seven kids in three states, and he never sees 'em. (*Brief pause.*)

RUBY: He must've kept saying "Yes, dear," right up till he left. (*Dad laughs. Relieved laughter from all but Rafe - he's partly relieved, partly disappointed. As silence falls again, Dad abruptly shoves Ruby off his knee, speaks to Ruby, Lance and Jackie, indicating Rafe.*)

DAD: This one's left the Army. Guess he's got a better idea how to make a living around here than the rest of us.

RAFE: No. But I know what I want.

MOM: You hear that, Ruby? Somebody around here knows. Ruby don't know *what* she wants, she just knows she ain't got it.

RUBY: (*Coolly.*) I'll know what I want when I see it.

DAD: (*Laughs.*) That's my girl.

JULIE: (*To Rafe:*) What *do* you want?

RAFE: (*To her, but for Dad to hear.*) Same thing I always did. And in the desert...all that time to think....now I got a plan.

DAD: Holy Jesus, Rafe, how'd I know it was you if you didn't have a plan? (*Laughter, mostly sympathetic.*)

RAFE: I want to get Granddad's farm going again. (*Silence falls. Plowing on:*) I thought it through this time. I got a little money saved, and I'm a veteran, I can get a loan and give you a down payment on the land and the old farmhouse - (*Julie touches his arm. Ignoring her, continuing:*) and I'm gonna buy a team of drafthorses and use 'em to farm, and do farmwork for other folks, haul timber and plow and do their haying -

Mary Gallagher

DAD: We work with machines around here -

RAFE: I think there are other folks who'd rather use horses, like me. And I'll do odd jobs too, work up to the lumber yard, deliver stuff, whatever needs doing to bring a little money in -

DAD: Aw hell, why don't you say you'll make barrel hoops and sell 'em from a wagon? - that's the way you're talking.

RAFE: It ain't just me - there are lots of folks who've gone back to farming the old way, all around the country -

DAD: Yeah, and they all got their heads up their asses. They think chickens are cute cause they never had to get to know no chickens, and find out they're the dumbest, meanest critters out in nature. There ain't one of 'em that grew up on a farm like I did, where you had to git up every goddamn morning of your life before it was even light, to milk them goddamn cows - and if I overslept, my dad just come and threw me out of bed, and he was right to do it - cause winter, summer, Sundays, Christmas, it wasn't no different, there was the same chores to be done. And you had more chores *off* the farm - cause even if your whole family worked till your guts ached, you couldn't make your ends meet unless you had a couple of you working off the farm. You grow up on a farm, you got no romance about farming. You shoulda stuck it out in the Army, boy.

RAFE: It can work, and I'm gonna do it, if you'll sell me the farm.

DAD: (*Beat; then:*) I told you to quit thinking of that years ago.

JULIE: (*To Rafe, defiantly breaking rules:*) He sold it off, Rafe. (*Silence. Rafe looks at his father, who ignores him, takes another shot.*)

RAFE: ...You sold off Granddad's land while I was gone?

JULIE: The house, too. All of it.

DAD: (*To Julie:*) When did you join this family? (*As she flushes, to Rafe:*) I don't answer to you, boy. But I'll tell you this, all my life, I never had two nickels to rub together, no more'n my dad did, till I give up on farming. When I went to work for the county highway department, that's when we started paying bills regular around her.....aw hell, ain't nobody even offered to farm that land in 20 years -

RAFE: I offered! You knew I always wanted it -

DAD: That was a ro-mance, boy. Ruby, talk some sense into your brother -

RAFE: Who'd you sell it to? (*Dad makes a disgusted gesture, starts to exit.*) *Who was it?*

DAD: (*Over his shoulder, exiting:*) I'm going to bed - some of us gotta work tomorrow. (*Dad and Mom exit, leaving Rafe with Julie, Ruby, Lance and Jackie - his sister, girl, best friends. Beat, then:*)

RAFE: ALL my life...

JULIE: I know.

RUBY: I know, but Dad...he sees it different...

JACKIE: Yeah, that old-style farming...I always liked your idea of it. But when it comes to push and shove...

LANCE: Yeah, pretty tough row to hoe, Rafe...

RAFE: Nobody believed me.

JULIE: I believed you. (*Under his steady gaze, she weakens.*)...I mean, I knew you always really wanted it...

RAFE: Did you think I could *do* it?

JULIE: (*Weaker yet.*)...If your dad woulda let you... (*Rafe gives a short bitter laugh, turns away, looks at Ruby.*)

RUBY: It's a guy from the city. Evan Brooks, his name is. Not too old either - maybe thirty. Kinda good-looking, in a way.

LANCE: Oh, yeah? (*Lance tries to drop an arm on Ruby's shoulder. She shrugs it off, goes on to Rafe:*)

RUBY: I only seen him twice, he hardly ever comes up here. Don't know why he bought it. (*Beat; then:*) Are you gonna do something?

RAFE: I ain't gonna let it go.

RUBY: You better be careful, Rafe.

RAFE: You against me too?

RUBY:...I'm just saying...Dad could still hurt you if he wanted to -

RAFE: Not no more, he can't.

Crossfade as they exit, Rafe in one direction, the others in another. Darlene in the Mom mask enters, addresses the audience.

MOM: He talks like he hates farming, but you notice we still got the biggest garden on the road, with the farmstand out front, where we sell off what we don't eat or put up for the winter. The garden and the stand, that's my work, mostly - and Ruby when I can catch ahold of her - but he acts like he hates all that. Every fall he says, "Aw hell, let's not even plow up the field next year." But then come spring, he says, "Aw hell, might's well put something in the ground." See, he can change his mind. If that Brooks from the city hadn't made his offer when he did, right after the tax bill come...or if Marlin hadn't heard about the Harrises up in the Vly selling off their pastureland for fifty thousand dollars...(*Pause. She shrugs.*) But see, Rafe wanted him to keep the land for Rafe...to have that be his reason. And he never woulda done that. He don't feel that way about life. Life is hard. Mostly you don't get what you want. But you take it and you keep your mouth shut and you do the best you can. Mostly he's been a good husband to me. And when he ain't...mostly I don't hold them times against him. But one time comes back up on me. I was sick, and the kids was sick, and it was hard winter, Marlin was out there with the county snowplows fourteen hours a day, and coming home when he could and taking care of us. He didn't say nothing about it, that ain't his way. But one night when he finally laid down to sleep, the cat was sick right there under our bed. And Marlin, he got right up and cleaned up the cat-sick, and then he got dressed again. He took that cat, Alice her name was, and he drove off with her. When he come back, he didn't have no cat. I didn't say nothing...I could see how he come to do it...but she was *my* cat.

(*Beat; then:*) If she'da been Rafe's cat, it woulda been the same. Now, Ruby's cat...I don't believe he woulda done that way.

Crossfade Dylan enters with his shirt off, starts chopping wood. Mom watches him for a long moment, then exits. Ruby enters, carrying a large, full shoulder bag. She approaches Dylan's spot, not looking at him - she's walking along the road that passes downstage of Dylan. The farmhouse is behind Dylan a big meadow is across the road, in the direction of the audience. Dylan looks at her, stops work. Ruby keeps walking throughout dialogue, till indicated.

DYLAN: Hey.

RUBY: (*Glances vaguely at him.*) Hey.

DYLAN: Hey, hold on a minute.

RUBY: Why?

DYLAN: Why not?

RUBY: I gotta go to work.

DYLAN: Where?

RUBY:(*Smiling.*) Why?

DYLAN:(*Smiling.*) Why not? (*Ruby has passed him - now she turns, whisks a McDonald's cap out of her bag, puts it on her head, walking backward.*) McDonald's? That's way out in Lindaville.

RUBY: I know it is. I gotta catch my ride.

DYLAN: I've got a truck, I'll take you. (*Ruby stops walking at last, coolly considers this.*)

RUBY: You're not from around here.

DYLAN: Nope. Caretaking this place for the guy who owns it. He can vouch for me.

RUBY: He ain't around much.

DYLAN: (*Grins.*) No, it works out great. (*Ruby smiles back, but still considers. Not worried, Dylan waits a beat, then, low-key and charming:*) It's beautiful land, isn't it? Especially this meadow across the road. You just picture horses in it. And this old house is falling down, but it's got style. I'll be sorry if he tears it down.

RUBY: (*Thrown by that suggestion.*)...My granddad was born in it.

DYLAN: (*Even more intrigued.*)...I'll go get the truck.

Still in the cap, she watches him exit. Crossfade as Darlene enters with a grocery bag stuffed with her McDonald's uniform. She takes it out as Ruby takes hers out of her shoulder bag. They change into their uniforms as they talk.

DARLENE: Where'd you go last night? We thought you was coming out to the dirt track.

RUBY: Didn't feel like it.

DARLENE: Lance was looking for you. He looked good too, got his ear pierced in three places! Had little gold rings in, he looked so cool.

RUBY: (*Amused.*) That ain't gonna go over too good at the lumber yard.

DARLENE: Lisa was hanging on him, I'm serious. He won all his races too.

RUBY: (*Dismissive gesture like her father's.*) Aw hell, he always wins the quarter-mile, since he was twelve or something. Why don't he move up to the half-mile and go for it?

DARLENE: Why do you give him such a bad time? I wish Dale ever treated me half as nice as Lance treats you.

RUBY: I wouldn't take the shit you take from Dale, Darlene. And you don't have to, either.

DARLENE: Well...I got Ashley to think of now...

RUBY: You always took shit from him.

DARLENE:...He don't mean it...

RUBY: What *does* he mean? One of these days he's gonna run you down in the parking lot in that stupid high-wheeler he went and bought.

DARLENE: Do you want Lance or not?

RUBY: (*Long beat; then:*) You ever read the wedding announcements in the *BANNER*?

DARLENE:...We don't take a paper regular -

RUBY: (*Affectionate.*) Yeah, you only read the *STAR*.

DARLENE: Hey, when I buy the *STAR*, you read the whole thing -

RUBY: Yeah, but you believe it.

DARLENE:...Well, it's right there in black and white, why wouldn't it be true?

RUBY: Darlene...

DARLENE: Well, I spose you don't believe the wedding announcements either.

RUBY: I believe 'em, that's what's wrong with 'em. "The bride is a medical receptionist. The bridegroom is a shipping clerk at Sears. After a honeymoon in Florida, they are living in Lindaville."

DARLENE: Wish Dale was a shipping clerk at Sears.

RUBY: "The bridegroom is a plumber's assistant in Crawley. The bride is a clerk at the Crawley Laundromat. After a honeymoon in the Poconos, they are living in Crawley."

DARLENE: I bet I'll never in my whole life see the Poconos with

Dale! But Lance would take you anywhere, if you'd just not spit on him -

RUBY: He likes it when I spit on him - but you're missing the point, Darlene. Is that all they're gonna get? Probably get pregnant on their stupid boring honeymoon, and forever after they'll be "living in Lindaville?" Don't that depress you?

DARLENE: Yeah, they depress me cause they're so much better off than me.

RUBY:...I give up.

DARLENE:...You're just spoiled is all. (*Ruby looks at her. Darlene nods wisely. Ruby smiles, starts playing with Darlene's hair, twisting it around various ways in front of the mirror as Darlene lights a cigarette. During this*)

RUBY:...Maybe.

DARLENE: Are you seeing somebody besides Lance?

RUBY: I ain't seeing Lance.

DARLENE: You know what I mean. (*Pause. Ruby drops Darlene's hair.*)

RUBY:...I don't know what I'm doing yet...

DARLENE: (*Ponytails her hair.*) Well, you seem all stirred up to me.

RUBY: I'm *alive.*

Ruby exits. Darlene grabs both her bag and Ruby's, follows Ruby out. Crossfade to Rafe at a worktable, trying to rebuild the carburetor of an old pick-up truck, using small wrenches and screwdrivers to remove and replace the jets. This is hot, greasy, painstaking work. Dylan as Dad passes, carrying a sack lunch and a thermos, stops a little distance from Rafe.

DAD: What you doing there?

RAFE: Gonna get that truck going.

DAD: (*Wryly amused.*) Well, I hope Jesus Christ and Moses and all the twelve apostles is gonna come down and piss on that truck, cause that's what it'll take to get her going again.

RAFE: (*Eyes on his work.*) I'll get her going. (*Dad makes his disgusted gesture, but doesn't leave. Beat; then:*)

DAD: Well, you don't give up easy, I'll say that for ya.(*Brief pause. Then, still not looking at Dad:*)

RAFE: I'm moving out.

DAD: Good. What kept ya?

RAFE: (*Beat; then:*) You can still cut me deep, you old son of a bitch. (*Dad regrets his words but can't say so. So...*)

DAD: Who you calling old? (*Rafe looks at him for the first time in the scene, then gives a small, sour laugh. Beat; then*) I ain't saying I know how to talk to you or ever did.

RAFE: That's for damn sure.

DAD: Aw shut up. (*Brief pause.*) I gotta go to work. And you better get your tail out and find yourself a job.

RAFE: I told you what I'm gonna do, I'm gonna get that land back -

DAD: Now just don't talk so goddamn stupid, Rafe. Do what you can do in the world, and don't go getting tangled up in fairytales. (*No answer. Approaching the table, Dad sets down the sack, opens the thermos, saying:*) You want a little pick-me-up?

RAFE: (*Expressionless.*) No, thanks.

DAD: There's coffee in it too, for all you know. (*No answer. Dad pours coffee-whiskey mix into the thermos cup, drinks, then:*) I'm gonna give you some of Granddad's land.

RAFE: (*Stunned beat; then:*) I thought you sold it all.

DAD: The farmland and the pastureland, I did. But there's all that other land leading up to hunting camp. Close to fifty acres. I'll give you ten.

RAFE: (*Beat; then:*) I couldn't farm that land.

DAD: Hell, no. Your granddad used to say, "It's so steep back there, you'd have to harness the thunder and lightning to haul 'em up top." (*Chuckles.*)

RAFE: What good is it?

DAD:...It's family land. Build a cabin, where our old hunting cabin used to be before they burned it down, whoever them bastards was...

RAFE: I'm gonna farm.

DAD:...He's gonna farm....well, goodness to mercy, you go ahead and do that. You break your back cutting down and hauling trees, and hauling stones, and clearing out the poison ivy and the nettles and the skunks and snakes...it's your land, you have yourself a time, suffering all over it. (*Dad starts out. Rafe stops him by saying:*)

RAFE: I ain't gonna farm it. But I'll take it. (*Dad looks at him, maybe hoping for some connection. Rafe regards him stonily.*)

DAD: "Never give a inch," that's you, ain't it?

RAFE: It is now. (*Dad makes his disgusted gesture, goes.*

Crossfade to Dylan entering with a small tree with its roots in burlap, and a shovel. He sets them down, flops on the ground, bone-tired. Rafe enters from another direction, wary but drawn.)

RAFE: 'Lo.

DYLAN:...Hey, how ya doing?

RAFE: You're planting trees here?

DYLAN: Right.

RAFE:...My family's been clearing this land for a hundred years. Now you're planting trees on it.

DYLAN: Oh, you're Ruby's brother? I'm Dylan. (*Pause - no recognition from Rafe, so...*) They aren't my idea, the trees - I just work for him.

RAFE: What the hell's he want more trees for?

DYLAN: Investment. Tax thing. Using the land for business purposes, raising trees to sell.

RAFE: We're sitting in the middle of a forest.

DYLAN: Guess the IRS guys don't know that. Or don't care.

RAFE: What else is he gonna do?

DYLAN: Says he wants to make a pond down there in the meadow.

RAFE: A pond? What for?

DYLAN: (*Shrugs.*) Swim in it? Look at it? Increase the resale value? It'd be too bad, that stream that runs through the meadow is full of spotted turtles. They wouldn't make it in a pond.

RAFE:...You mean them mud turtles. I seen 'em since I was a kid.

DYLAN:...Is that what you call 'em here?

RAFE: That meadow oughta have horses ln it.

DYLAN: That's what I say too. But some guys can't just buy the land and sit on it. They gotta rearrange it. This guy I work for, Brooks, seems like an okay guy, but he hardly ever comes up here, and when he does, he sits out on the back porch for fifteen minutes, and he gets the backhoe itch. If he could buy up the whole county, he'd move Slide Mountain, put it on the other side of Hightop.

RAFE: (*Warming up.*) You're not from these parts.

DYLAN: Nope. But I like it around here. Like it the way it is.

RAFE: If I had my way, none of the crap that come in since I was a kid'd be here.

DYLAN:...Yeah well, sure -

RAFE: I'd like to see trees growing up through the K-Mart parking lot.

DYLAN:(*Laughs.*) Right...right...

RAFE: I gotta talk to him before he starts bringing them backhoes in...you know Ruby?

DYLAN: ...Yeah, ah-huh...

Rafe looks at him another beat; then, not pursuing that:

RAFE: See that ridge up there above the stand of pine trees?

DYLAN: ...Yeah...

RAFE: That's where I'm living right now. You can find me there and let me know when he comes up again.

DYLAN: Okay.

RAFE: I'm gonna buy that meadow back, keep my horses in it.

DYLAN: Great! What kind of horses have you got?

RAFE: Ain't got 'em yet.

DYLAN: Oh...

RAFE: Not yet. But I will. (*He exits, leaving Dylan half-amused, half-disconcerted: strange guy, Ruby's brother.*)

Crossfade to Rafe's camp, night. Rafe and Julie emerge from the shadows, Rafe leading the way. Rafe carries a flashlight and a pail of water. Juliewears shorts and sandals, carries a tote bag, is getting bitten by mosquitoes and tripping over rocks and tree roots.

JULIE: (*Tripping.*) Shit!

RAFE: Why'd ya wanta wear them shoes?

JULIE: How'd *I* know it'd be this rough...there's hardly a trail, even.

RAFE: That's why my dad give me the land. He can't sell it 'cause it's on the backside of a mountain, nobody in his right mind'd trouble to build on it.

JULIE: (*Rueful love.*) But that ain't stopping you.

RAFE: I ain't building here. I'm just squatting, temporary. You know where I'm gonna build.

JULIE: In the meadow.

RAFE: Sure. Well, on the rise...looking down on the meadow. I wanta be able to see that big old rock and them two little branches of the creek from my bedroom window. (*Pause.*) You want something to drink?

JULIE: Okay. (*Slaps mosquitoes.*)

RAFE: Got Coke and 7-Up in the stream there, keeps it nice and cold. Got a watermelon too.

JULIE: You hauled a watermelon up here? (*He just looks at her, so...*)...How 'bout a beer?

RAFE: Don't keep it around.

JULIE: One beer ain't gonna hurt you, Rafe.

RAFE: You know my dad, you know why I'd rather not get into it.

JULIE:...I'll take a Coke. (*Slaps mosquitoes.*)

RAFE: Put some of that bug stuff on, it's in my pack.

JULIE:...I don't want to smell like that tonight...

Mary Gallagher

RAFE: Okay, get bit. (*He exits.*)

Crossfade to another part of the stage. Ruby and Dylan sit on the floor of an otherwise empty room in the old farmhouse. Moonlight pours through a window.

RUBY: Tell me some more about your travels. Tell about that old hotel with the birds.

DYLAN: I'm gonna run out of stories pretty soon.

RUBY: You better not.

DYLAN: Oh, that's all you're coming around for, huh?

RUBY: (*Looks at him; then, leaving him hanging:*) What's your favorite place you've ever been?

DYLAN:...The next place.

RUBY: (*Delighted.*) Yeah? Where'll that be?

DYLAN: Won't know till I get there.

RUBY: (*Laughs, excited.*) That's it, that's what I want!

DYLAN: Why not? (*They smile: powerful connection. Ruby turns away.*)

RUBY: Funny, being up here. I used to play in here when I was little. And my dad likes to talk to me about it, sometimes...how it was when he was growing up in this old house, and even what it musta been like way back in the old days, when my great-great-grandparents homesteaded here. They had twenty-two kids in this house. I don't know where they put 'em all...Well, a lot of 'em died, though.

DYLAN: Yeah?...maybe they're still around.

RUBY:...Where, here?

DYLAN: Perfect place for it. Empty house. Sold off to a stranger.

They're gonna hang around till the one true rightful family is living in the house again.

RUBY: They're gonna get tired of waiting.

DYLAN: Sssshhhh... you'll get 'em all riled up. (*Ghostlike.*) Wooooooooooo . . .

RUBY: (*Laughs.*) Quit that, you!...

DYLAN: Doesn't it bother you?

RUBY: (*Dismissive.*) What, ghosts?

DYLAN: Losing your family's house and land. It sure bothers your brother.

RUBY:...A little bit, I guess...but my dad's right, land that don't make money is just a stone around your neck. Let somebody else pay the taxes.

DYLAN: Right, right...

RUBY: Anyway, who wants to farm? You can't never get away! Dad says when this whole county was nothing but farmers, and a killing frost was coming, the church bells would ring in the middle of the night, and people would get out of bed and gather all the blankets and clothes in the whole house to cover up the crops, so they wouldn't all die that same night. Farmers gotta be around all the time for stuff like that. I ain't gonna get stuck like that, nowhere, nohow, no way. I'm gonna go everywhere, see everything...like you.

DYLAN:...Well, don't leave just yet, okay?

RUBY: ...Same to you. (*A long, almost challenging look between them. Abruptly, Ruby kisses him.*)

Crossfade to Rafe and Julie. Rafe returns with two bottles of Coke, gives one to Julie.

RAFE: Maybe I'll make a fire. Keep the bugs off.

Mary Gallagher

JULIE: That'd be nice. (*Rafe hauls firewood, builds a fire. Julie watches him start this action. Silence grows. Finally:*)

JULIE: I got promoted.

RAFE: Good for you.

JULIE: My boss says I've got a real future there. Says he's lucky to have me.

RAFE: Smart guy.

JULIE: So I asked him would he pay for me to take some courses at the CC -

RAFE: At the what?

JULIE: The community college...and he said he would. So in the fall I'm gonna go to school three nights a week. I'm gonna take advanced computer science and statistics and French.

RAFE: You're on your way, sounds like.

JULIE: That's right, I am. I don't want to live in a trailer all my life.

RAFE: Your folks done the best they could.

JULIE: People ain't meant to live in trailers, Rafe. Not in America.

RAFE: Hey, I ain't blaming you. You're doing what you gotta do for yourself, just like I am. I respect you, you know that.

JULIE: (*Beat; then:*) I brought you some stuff, here...(*Fishes in her shoulder bag.*)

RAFE: (*Gentle teasing.*) Uh-oh. It ain't candy and cookies and razor blades, is it?

JULIE: Shut up. It's food, though...I just thought...you roughing it out here...maybe I'd bring you something special... (*Julie spreads out a cloth near the fire that Rafe is building, lays on it small, pretty* *paper plates and matching napkins, grapes, a little cheese knife, a box of fancy French crackers and slabs of cheese wrapped in cellophane. Meanwhile:*)

RAFE: This ain't so rough. Had it a whole lot rougher when I hunted with my dad. Up here, I got a latrine, even. Dug it myself. Only thing they taught me in the Army that come in handy. Had to dig it twice, though. Spent all day digging a eight-feet hole and then I didn't cover it and it rained all night. Filled up the whole damn hole in one damn night. Had to dig another one just to get even... Now don't you never tell that story on me. If my dad come to hear about it, he'd tell it on me every day till the day he died. (*He kneels to light the fire - FIRELIGHT LIGHTING EFFECT - looks at the food. Puzzled, he picks up the cracker box.*)

RAFE:...What are they getting at here?

JULIE: It's in French. They're French crackers.

RAFE:...Uh-huh...(*Picks up cheese slab, hefts it in his hand.*)

JULIE: That's French cheese too. Brie, that one is. It's real good.

RAFE: Looks pretty well cooked down, here, Julie.

JULIE: That's how it's supposed to look .

RAFE:...Well, at least it ain't pre-sliced in them little envelopes.

JULIE: This is the classy stuff! I would've brought some wine, they always have wine with their meals in France, but I figured you wouldn't drink it.

RAFE: You figured right. Where'd you get wine, anyway? You ain't twenty-one.

JULIE:...I can get it when I want to.

RAFE: From your boss, or who? (*No answer. He picks up another cheese.*) This one must be a reject - it ain't runny.

JULIE: It ain't the runny type - it's chevre.

RAFE:"Shevrah"...(*Opening cellophane to sniff.*) What's in it?

JULIE:(*Reluctant.*)...Goat cheese - but it's good, go on and try it - !

RAFE:(*Laughs.*) Goat cheese! Hell, my grandma used to make that stuff and us kids wouldn't eat it. We played with them goats, we *knew* 'em! They'd eat anything from poison ivy to chicken shit -

JULIE: Well, fine! You can spend the rest of your life living in a tent and eating Ritz crackers!

RAFE:(*Opening cheese, smelling it.*) Nothing wrong with Ritz crackers. Charlton Heston eats 'em. You're the one that told me that.

JULIE: Well, I can't live my life on Ritz crackers! I gotta go to work in an office every day, and I gotta look my best! I gotta wear nice stockings that don't have ladders in 'em, not to mention twigs and burrs - and I gotta blow dry my hair and put my makeup on -

RAFE: All for this boss of yours? Lotta trouble, seems to me -

JULIE: It's for him and me and everyone who's living out there in the world in 1991! This is how people live, Rafe! And I can't do all the stuff I gotta do, if I have to sleep in a tent and piss in a latrine and hike a two-mile trail just to get to my car, can I?

RAFE: Who asked you to? (*Julie starts to cry. Shocked, Rafe stares, not knowing what to do. Long beat, then:*)...Julie, I'm just teasing ya...(*Awkwardly touches her.*)

JULIE: I thought...I thought you...

RAFE:...What?

JULIE: You know!...I thought you...wanted me around...

RAFE:...I do...

JULIE:...All the time, I mean...

RAFE:...Well...I got things to do, I got a hard row to hoe, and -

JULIE: You're making it a hard row! You don't have to do all this - you could do anything! Rafe, all's we gotta do is get on the same road together - we can have a real good life cause the opportunities are out there, I just know it! (*Rafe can't answer - he doesn't want the life she wants. He keeps stroking her back. She looks at him, knowing why he doesn't answer - arguing is futile. She's calmer now, but deeply unhappy. Finally, still stroking her, gently:*)

RAFE: D'I tell you I bought a team of draft horses?

JULIE:...You told me. (*Beat; then:*) I shouldn'ta waited for you.

RAFE: Don't say that ...I'm glad you waited. (*Beat; he embraces her.*)

Crossfade to Evan Brooks, played by Jackie in a mask, entering the porch of the old farmhouse - a couple of old wicker chairs and a small table. Dylan hurries out of the house to meet him. Brooks is arriving from the city, has an expensive overnight case and a mid-size brown paper bag, dangles car keys. Dylan is surprised and flustered, but strives for his usual ease and charm.

DYLAN: Hi, Mr. Brooks, good to see ya -

BROOKS: Place looks better already, Dylan. Even in the dark. I see you got those trees in.

DYLAN: Yeah, they look real nice, too. Can I help you, have you got some other stuff - ?

BROOKS: Nah, this is it, I'm just here overnight. Got a van coming up with some furniture tomorrow. Can you be around for that?

DYLAN: Oh sure, no problem.

BROOKS:(*Sets brown bag on table.*) Great. You know, we never talked about your hours when I'm up here.

DYLAN: Oh, well...fine, whatever...

BROOKS:(*Taking deli food out of the bag.*) Well, usually I'd say you can take off most of the time I'm here, go visit friends, stay all

Mary Gallagher

night, have fun...I'd like the privacy too, frankly...

DYLAN: (*Uneasy - where would he go?*) Ohh...oh, sure...

BROOKS:...but this van is coming pretty early in the morning. (*Starts doctoring a sandwich from little tubes of condiments.*) Oops...I'm making kind of a mess here -

DYLAN: You want a plate or something? And napkins? I could -

BROOKS: No, I'll get it - I think I left some beer here too - (*Brooks starts for the house door. Dylan gets in his path, eager to beat him to the door.*)

DYLAN: Yeah, you did, three bottles - no, really, let me get it - I gotta admit, I got a few dishes piled up in there -(*Ruby comes out of the house. She wears her big T-shirt and nothing else, looks like she just got out of bed. She's embarrassed, but has decided to carry it off, and does.*)

RUBY: Hi, Mr. Brooks. I'm here too.(*Brooks is surprised, amused, impressed with Ruby. He handles it with aplomb.*)

BROOKS: Oh...oh, okay, hello...(*Shakes hands.*) Evan Brooks.

RUBY: Ruby Carroll. My dad sold you this house.

BROOKS: (*Overlapping Ruby.*)...I've seen you, but we haven't met...well, nice to meet you, Ruby.

RUBY: I ain't been in this old house in a lotta years. When my granddad got too old and sick and he moved in with us, my dad closed this house up. I was kinda glad to hear somebody bought it...maybe even have kids playing in it again.

BROOKS: Not mine. I mean, I'm not married.

DYLAN: Ruby wanted to look around the old place -

BROOKS: Sure, sure. Any time...Well, I'm going to get a beer. Ruby, would you like...?

RUBY: Oh, sure.

BROOKS: Dylan?

DYLAN: Uh . . .sure, thanks a lot... (*Brooks goes out. Dylan and Ruby wait a beat, then give each other "Oh my God!" looks, trying not to laugh.Whispers*) I don't believe this, you've got him waiting on you!

RUBY:(*Pretended offhand.*) Why don't you believe it? (*He laughs silently, proud of her, reaches for her - she grins, evades him, sits in a wicker chair. More offhand yet*) I coulda combed my hair, I guess...(*Dylan loves this. Brooks comes back out with beers. Dylan quickly takes two, hands one to Ruby.*)

DYLAN: Thanks a lot. Want me to get that plate for you - ?

BROOKS: No, I'll eat later - I need to relax.

RUBY: Well, you come to the right place. It's so relaxing around here, you're likely to fall asleep at the wheel.

BROOKS:(*Amused.*) Tired of country life?

RUBY: What life? There ain't no life. There's the mall and the dirt track and the bowling alley, period. And skinny-dipping in the summer - that's the real big thrill.

BROOKS: ...But it's beautiful country.

RUBY: Yeah, well...trees is trees.

BROOKS: Sounds like you're a city girl. Get down there much?

RUBY: Couple times on high school trips, that's all. My mom and dad think it's the hell-and-damnationville.

BROOKS: Something to be said for that.

RUBY: Exciting, huh? Things changing every minute.

BROOKS:...Sometimes it kind of wears you out.

RUBY: Ain't nothing ever changes here, unless somebody's house burns down. I'll get down there one of these days. I bet I don't come back.

BROOKS: You should check it out first, before you burn your bridges. If you decide to come down for a visit, call me. I could show you around a little.

RUBY:(*Hiding her amazement.*) Oh...well...thanks...

BROOKS: Here, I'll give you my card.(*Stunned silence as he takes out his wallet, opens it - it's jammed with money and credit cards. Ruby and Dylsn try not to stare as Brooks takes out a card, hands it to Ruby.*) Give me a few weeks notice, things are hectic lately. But sure...might be nice to see the city through your eyes. Seems pretty grim to me these days...(*Silence falls. Dylan has been watching this interchange and is surprised to feel jealous. He wills Ruby to look at him. She doesn't - drinks her beer, stares into space as both men look at her. Long beat; then:*) Well. I've got more phone calls to make tonight. (*Hands Dylan his empty beer bottle, takes the food and exits, saying:*) See you in the morning, Dylan. Bright and early, right?

DYLAN: Right, right.

BROOKS:(*To Ruby:*)...Will I see you too - ?

DYLAN: Oh no, no, she's not living here or anything...(*Ruby gives Dylan a cool look, which is noted by both men.*)

RUBY:(*To Brooks:*) No, I'm not living here or *anything*.

BROOKS: Oh. Well...see you, then.(*Brooks goes out. Ruby swigs the last of her beer, not looking at Dylan. He watches Brooks out - silence. Then, very softly:*)

DYLAN: What was that?

RUBY: What was what?

DYLAN:"I'm not living her or *anything*," what was that - ?

RUBY: Well, how 'bout you? Acting like you had to apologize for me -

DYLAN: I was not apologizing, I was...

RUBY: Kissing his ass.

DYLAN: Like hell I was. I just...I need this job...

RUBY: I thought you was just passing through. (*Brief pause.*)

DYLAN: You're not gonna take him up on it, are you?

RUBY: Why not?

DYLAN:(*Beat; then:*) What would you want to do that for?

RUBY:(*Beat; then:*) Why not? (*Dylan looks at her a longer beat, starts to turn away toward the house, holding the beer bottles. Softly.*) Dylan.(*He turns back. She hands him her empty bottle. He takes it automatically, then has a flash of deep anger which she sees - instantly, she laughs, delighted at the successful teasing: gotcha, but with a note of playful apology too. Dylan looks at her a long beat, then gestures as if braining her with the empty bottle. Her laughter soars - she's on top of the world. Dylan tosses the empty bottles onto a cushioned chair.*)

DYLAN: I might have to drown you one of these days.

RUBY: I don't know as I'd blame ya. But I bet I swim better'n you do. (*He turns away, starts off. She jumps up, runs to catch him, holds him from behind, pressing close. They're motionless for a long beat. Then:*) I don't want you to go thinking this is easy.

DYLAN:(*Still motionless and angry.*)...No danger of that.

RUBY: I never slept with anyone before. I chose you.

DYLAN: Why?

RUBY:(*Moves around to face him. Very softly.*) Cause you got the magic. You're gonna get me out. (*He stares at her, then as if he can't help himself, he moves to kiss her. She pulls him down to the floor as:)*

DYLAN:(*Softly.*)...We can't do it here -

RUBY: He's busy making money, he won't bother us -

DYLAN: He's right upstairs -

RUBY: So? (*Dylan hesitates, very torn, afraid of losing her. Sitting on the floor, she looks him in the eye, reaches to pull her Tshirt off. He grabs her, pulls her up.*)

DYLAN: No! Come on. (*Dylan hurries Ruby off into darkness - they exit.*)

Crossfade to Mom, speaking to the audience.

MOM: She didn't know how good she had it. That's what I kept thinking. Even when she was little, she always had her way with men, making 'em go here and there, like she was driving team. She done it with her father, with her brother, with every stranger...(*Beat; then*) Marlin was the only one ever come looking out for me when I was a girl. And he wouldn't do *nothing* I wanted, wouldn't change his shoes for me, he'd come see me in his workboots, gunked up with manure and mud...but he wanted me. He was a handsome boy, and had his way of talking. Liked a beer, but he didn't show it then, how he would get to lean on it. And we had good times in them days. He built our house at night while he was working full days on the highway crew. He'd come home dog-tired and eat some supper and then start to work again, pouring cement or laying joists. Come dark, I'd hold the flashlight for him so he could see to work. Sometimes we'd be real close like that and he'd say, "Ceelie, put that flashlight down..." (*Beat; then*) But he was the only one. I woulda had to take him even if I hadn't liked him. And when Ruby come along...he just followed in her path...giving her her way...doing what she wanted, like he never would for me...(*Beat; then:*) And when I seen that boy along the road...I knew he'd do the same. He'd follow right in Ruby's path...and she'd be careless of him. (*Dylan enters, carrying a heavy piece of furniture. He stops just onstage, breathing hard, and sets it down heavily, some distance from the porch area. He isn't aware of Mom until she speaks. But* *she's acutely aware of him, struggles against a violent impulse, loses, blurts out:*)

MOM: Hey, you.

DYLAN: (*Looks, surprised.*) Oh, hi.

MOM: ...What you doing?

DYLAN:...Just hauling some furniture. (*Mom starts drawing closer to Dylan, very slowly and tentatively, moving unobtrusively closer on each line.*) Looks like thirsty work.

DYLAN: Yeah...kinda hot already.

MOM: (*Can't help herself, blurts awkwardly:*) Come on up to the house and have a cold drink.

DYLAN: (*Beat; then:*) The house?

MOM: Right up the road, there.

DYLAN:...Are you Ruby's mom?

MOM: (*Nods, reluctant.*) I'm Ceelie.

DYLAN: (*Puts out hand to shake.*) Nice to meet you, finally. I'm Dylan.

MOM: I know...pretty name. (*She takes his hand, stares down at their clasped hands as if shyly, but can't make herself let go.*)

DYLAN:...Is Ruby...? Ruby's not home, is she?

MOM: (*Still holding his hand.*) No. She's at work. So's her dad. It's real quiet up there...cool...I got cold things to drink. (*Dylan is thrown by her manner, but he can't believe Ruby's mother would come onto him, especially in this weird shy way, decides she's just very odd, detaches his hand, smiling.*)

DYLAN: Well...thanks a lot, but...my boss is here, he's sleeping but if he wakes up...It's really great to meet you, though. Ruby's great, she's...(*Brooks enters the porch area with a coffee mug. Mom sees him and instantly exits, thwarted, embarrassed, perhaps relieved, but trying to show none of it. Dylan calls after her as he goes to pick up furniture again:*) Thanks a lot! Sometime soon, I'd really like that...

BROOKS: (*To Dylan.*) Hold on a sec, I'll finish my coffee and give you a hand...who was that?

DYLAN: Ruby's mom.

BROOKS: (*Surprised.*) Really?...I wouldn't have figured that. Sure didn't take you long to find the prettiest girl around. Seems sure of herself, too...for someone that young...

DYLAN:...Yeah...

BROOKS: How old is she, do you know?

DYLAN:...Eighteen, seventeen, in there...

BROOKS:...Eighteen?...She'll be dangerous in a few years.

DYLAN:...Dangerous?

BROOKS: But she's too young yet, and too rough. The edges, I mean...

DYLAN: (*Relieved.*) Oh...well, yeah...

BROOKS: (*Abruptly.*) So if she does call me, I think I'll meet her in New York. Can't hurt, right?

DYLAN:...Sure, right...

BROOKS: I should probably talk to her parents about it. Let them know it's all highly respectable...I bet they watch her like a hawk.

DYLAN: I bet.

BROOKS: Do they?

DYLAN: Well...I don't know, really.

BROOKS: They'd be crazy not to. (*Dylan hesitates, very bothered by his inability to assert his rights where Ruby is concerned. Making that effort:*)

DYLAN: She's...I mean...we see each other, you know...(*Lamely.*) But I mean, she'd make up her own mind anyway.

BROOKS: That's the sense I have, too. (*Grins.*) Well, let's lug that thing inside. (*Brooks sets down his mug and strolls toward Dylan as Rafe enters just downstage of Dylan.*)

RAFE: (*To Dylan, soft, intense:*) You said you was gonna come and tell me when he showed up here.

DYLAN: (*Soft, annoyed.*) He got in late last night. You didn't expect me to climb up there in the dark, did you?

RAFE: I do it all the time.

DYLAN: Well...look, don't...(*As Rafe looks at him:*)...just take it easy, okay? (*Brooks reaches them, smiles at Rafe sticks out his hand.*)

RAFE: Rafe Carroll.

BROOKS: Evan Brooks. You're Ruby's brother?

RAFE:(*Looks at Dylan - back at Brooks.*) That's right, Mr. Evan, and I'll get right to the point. I got nothing against you, but I can't go along with my dad selling out the family land, to you or nobody.

BROOKS:...oh. Well...I can see that you might not appreciate -

RAFE: It ain't how I feel. It's what I'm gonna do. And you never met a guy more serious than me.

BROOKS:(*Glances at Dylan.*) Well...as I said, I can understand, but-

RAFE: Good, cause you and me can make this right. I can buy my own land back from you and you can sell it to me. (*Brief pause*.)

BROOKS:...Do you know what I paid your father for this property? It's over forty acres -

RAFE: You paid plenty for it or I don't know my dad. And I know I can't raise it all at once. But I'd like to start right now, and start with this here meadow. I got a team of draft horses, big beautiful animals, I want to turn 'em out to graze right here where they belong.

BROOKS:...Well...I really bought the property because of this meadow -

RAFE: Sure. And I don't wanta do you dirt, I'll pay a fair price for it, whatever my dad asked from you, plus something of a profit. How much would you take for it?

BROOKS:...For the meadow?

DYLAN: Yeah.

BROOKS:...I really couldn't sell it for less than a hundred thousand.

RAFE:(*Stares, speechless. Finally.*) It ain't even ten acres.

BROOKS: No, but I see it as the centerpiece of the whole property. I haven't decided whether I'm going to live on this property myself or develop it.

RAFE:...Develop it?

BROOKS: Oh, sure, this property has wonderful potential - especially the meadow, where the natural landscaping is lovely. If I had a pond dug in the middle and built three - four at the most houses around the pond...upscale housing, cedar shingles, cedar decks, local bluestone chimneys -

RAFE: The land boom is over, every highway and back road is nothing but "For Sale" signs!

BROOKS: In the long run, land values only rise. You just have to wait the rough times out. Your dad sold at a bad time. But I couldn't make the same mistake. This is my business, Rafe.

RAFE:...So you're gonna stick to that. A hundred thousand.

BROOKS: What would be rock-bottom. But I still couldn't sell it unless I felt sure that however *you* develop it, it would increase the value of the rest of the property.

RAFE: I ain't gonna develop beans. I'm gonna leave it whole.

BROOKS: Well, you'll use it for something, won't you?(*Rafe can't believe he has to explain to this stranger. He glances at the uncomfortable Dylan, who tries to remain blank-faced. Long beat; then:*)

RAFE: Graze my horses. Put a water trough in. Build a little stable. Might put a garden in, out toward the rise, with a stout fence around it to keep the horses out...in a couple years, put a little house up there...

BROOKS: Well, all that might be charming, or it might be an eyesore, depends on how you do it. As I said, I'm sympathetic, but this is what I do, and I can't do it badly just to make you feel better. I'm sure *you* understand *that*.

RAFE:...To a point, I do. (*Beat; then:*) Would you be willing to take a down payment and hold the mortgage?

BROOKS: Sorry, Rafe. It's just too shaky, especially in times like these. But I'll make you a deal. You raise the money and you draw up a specific proposal of how you'd use the land, and we'll talk about it. Okay? (*Claps Rafe on the back. To Dylan:*) Let's go. Heaveho. (*Brooks and Dylan pick up the furniture and head for the porch. Rafe stands motionless*).

Crossfade to Ruby and Darlene in the McDonald's parking lot, heading for work. They carry their usual uniforms-in-bags, wear their caps at rakish angles. Darlene is fervently smoking in the last seconds before she'll have to stub it out. As they amble toward the door:

RUBY: (*Absently, thoughts elsewhere.*)...You shoulda called the cops.

DARLENE: Oh, sure! Then how'd I raise the money to bail him out?...go around all begging to everybody who don't have no money to lend anyway...I know I oughta dump him, I know you're gonna say that, but...

RUBY: (*Vaguely.*) You gotta do what you gotta do. (*Puzzled, Darlene waits, then changes the subject.*)

DARLENE: You shoulda seen Lisa last night at the bar - she's got some french-fried nerve. Had her big old butt squeezed into them tight, shiny bicycle pants! And her hair looked like a rat sucked it.

RUBY:...Lisa ain't so bad. (*Lance appears. He's following Ruby, pretending not to, "casually" swigging a beer in a bag. Meanwhile:*)

DARLENE: Since when? Since you got tired of Lance?

RUBY: Lance ain't so bad either. They'll prob'ly be real good together.

DARLENE: Ruby, what the hell?

RUBY: We better get on into work -

DARLENE: What's going on? (*Ruby does her pretend-casual number, but her smile gives her away. Lance is watching and drawing near.*)

RUBY: I just feel good, is all.

DARLENE:...Well, shitsky-fitsky! (*As Ruby grins wider.*) It's that whoever-whatsit you've been seeing without admitting nothing lately - damn, I knew it! What's his name? When do I get to meet him? Damn! (*Ruby is laughing, shushing her, looks self-consciously around, sees Lance practically on top of them. She squeezes Darlene's arm.*) Ow! Shit! What - ?(*Darlene sees Lance. Beat; then:*)

RUBY: Hi.

DARLENE: Hi, Lance, how's it hanging?

LANCE: (*To Ruby:*) So what's his name?

RUBY:...Pardon me?

LANCE: Don't bother. I seen you with him.

RUBY:...What?

LANCE: I seen you in the woods with him. (*Ruby is embarrassed, defensive, clings to her cool as:*)

DARLENE: Lance, we gotta get into work -

LANCE: (*Right at Darlene*) So git. (*Darlene hesitates, looks at Ruby. Ruby shrugs coolly. Darlene stubs out her cigarette with her foot, saying:*)

DARLENE: The manager's prob'ly watching through the window there, you better hurry up. (*Darlene exits. Beat; then:*)

RUBY: So you've seen me with him. So?

LANCE: (*Beat; then:*) You treated me like shit.

RUBY: I don't owe you nothing. You're just my brother's friend -

LANCE: Don't give me that bullshit. Last summer, when I was kicking ass at the dirtrack every Saturday and taking home that prize money, you was damn proud to be with me - and I'm back winning every week now -

RUBY: I grew up since then. (*Beat; speechless, ready to explode, Lance swigs beer.*)

RUBY: The manager sees you drinking, he'll come out and run you off -

LANCE: Just let him try, I'll kick his head in.

RUBY: (*Beat; then:*) You got no call to be following me.

LANCE: That ain't how I see it. (*Beat; then, almost an appeal:*) I got a sponsor, Ruby.

RUBY: Who?

LANCE: Quincy's Tavern. They're gonna back me to move up to the half-mile track. And if I make it there, I can go out on the circuit! No more dragging some ole wreck out of the woods and building her from the ground up, just so's I could race...knowing I never had no chance at the half-mile track, cause the high-dollar cars'd win it even if their drivers couldn't drive a nail...A custom-built car, Ruby! Gonna go to driving school and learn all them techniques I can't learn on my own, cause nobody I ever seen up close knows shit...now I can show what I can do!

RUBY: (*Impressed inspite of herself.*)...Well, that's great...

LANCE: And you're the one kept telling me I had to move up or die. Well, now I'm moving up. And you...you can come along.

RUBY: You sure about this, Lance? You seen their money yet?

LANCE:...We shook on it. They can't go back on me.

RUBY: Well...I mean, Quincy's Tavern...they ain't much. How they gonna come up with enough money for all that stuff? You're hanging your hat on a small peg if you count on them -

LANCE: Shut up, now! (*Beat; then:*) That's your old man talking in your mouth. That ain't you talking, Ruby. (*Touching her.*)...If you stood by me...Ruby...I think about you...

RUBY: Don't. Just don't think about me. Pretty soon, I will be outa here. And Lisa, she'll be good for you -

LANCE: You ain't going nowhere.

RUBY: (*Long beat; then, coolly:*) I ain't afraid of you. (*She turns to go. He grabs her arm, hurting her. Ruby gasps, is motionless as Lance, behind her, leans close.*)

LANCE: (*In her ear.*) What if I had my gun? (*Darlene races out, in* *uniform, screaming:*)

DARLENE: Lance, you git on outa here, the manager's calling the cops! (*Darlene tries to pry Lance's fingers from Ruby's arm and can't. Ruby still hasn't moved. Darlene continues*) You git! Come on, let go now, git! The cops are coming, I ain't kidding (*Lance shoves Darlene away, hard enough to scare her. Then, still holding Ruby, he leans forward and kisses the back of her neck. Ruby doesn't move. Lance lets go of her, exits. When he's offstage:*) Jesus! Did he hurt ya?

RUBY: (*Shaken, shakes head no.*) Was everybody watching?

DARLENE: Are you kidding? All them golden-agers like to fall outa their plastic chairs! You're gonna have a bruise - I know. You want a smoke? Or else I got that peach schnapps hid in by the frying vats-

RUBY: (*Shakes head no.*) Let's git on in.

They head Offstage. Crossfade to Rafe:'s camp, night. Jackie and Rafe are sitting by the fire. Rafe is in a bleak, dark mood. Jackie has a beer and is munching something. He swallows. Silence. Then:

JACKIE: Want some more of that brie cheese?

RAFE: Naw.

JACKIE: It ain't too bad with Ritz Crackers. (*No answer. Beat; then:*) Ain't you got a radio up here?

RAFE: I like to hear the woods sounds.

JACKIE: Too loud. Sounds like them katydids got it in for us. (*Beat; then:*) Hey, want to hike down, hit a couple bars? You don't gotta drink or nothing. Have a coke, sleep on my ole couch - It's butt-sprung, but it's better than a sleeping bag -

RAFE: I like it up here. (*Brief pause.*)

JACKIE: Some folks think you're gonna get tired of this.

RAFE: They don't know me. (*Brief pause.*)

JACKIE: I ain't saying nothing...but the nights are getting cold already. What you gonna do come winter? (*Longer pause. Then*)

RAFE: My dad told me one time when he was a kid, Granddad drove a team up here when the snow was so deep it took him half a day to make it to the cabin. And it was deep cold, too. But Granddad come ahead, cause he was gonna meet his crew and help 'em do some logging. And my Dad come along. He said it was so durn cold, he was afraid he'd freeze to death sitting in the wagon, but he knew my Granddad and he never said a word. When they got to the cabin, wasn't nobody around logging, and come to find out they was all huddled up inside the cabin, burning all the wood. Said it was too durn cold to work. Granddad was so disgusted, he took and threw a load of wood up on the wagon and told my Dad to climb aboard and they went right straight back. (*Pause.*)

JACKIE: Julie coming by tonight?

RAFE: Not if she's got her stockings on. (*Beat; then:*) She's going out, some. Playing the field. I told her to. (*Beat; then:*) Lance might come by, though -

JACKIE: Naw, he started drinking early. Prob'ly smashing mail boxes with a baseball bat. (*Beat; then*) Well, maybe I'll get going - (*Sound Offstage of a high-powered rifle shot, very close. Rafe and Jackie hit the ground. Another rifle shot. They yell at the same time:*)

JACKIE: Hey, we're here, quit shooting!

RAFE: Hey, get outa here with that gun, there's folks living up here! (*A moment's silence, then as Rafe starts to rise, another blast, louder and closer. He hits the ground again.*)

JACKIE: HEY, GET THE FUCK OUT OF HERE!!!... (*They listen. Sound of branches crunching underfoot.*)

JACKIE:...He ain't going away.

RAFE:...Some asshole trying to prove something...

JACKIE: Nobody comes up here except folks we know. Nobody else knows the trail is even here.

RAFE: A trail's a trail. Too many people know about this place. (*Another rifle blast, closer..*)

JACKIE: GET OUTA HERE, YA FUCKING MORON, OR WE'LL FUCKING KILL YA! (*Rifle blast, closer yet.*) Jesus, who *is* that guy?...Think maybe some psycho escaped from the prison? (*Looks at Rafe.*) Ain't nobody got a burr up their butt about you...?

RAFE:(*Looks at him, beat, deadpan:*) Just my dad. (*Jackie laughs nervously, then screams as Lance roars into camp, shrieking a wild, prolonged, drunken cry and waving his high-powered rifle. In his crazed, drunken state, he falls over Rafe and Jackie, rolls to his feet, staggering, points the gun just above their heads and fires. The gun goes off BLAM!...shocking all three of them. A moment of stunned silence, then:*)

LANCE: (*Starts laughing.*)...Whoa, shit...(*Rafe grabs Lance's gun with one hand and shoves Lance away with the other as Jackie screams at Lance.*)

JACKIE: "Shit?"...you...you shit-for-brains! What the fuck are you doing here?!

LANCE:...I just miscounted one, I thought It was empty...chill out, you ain't hurt none...(*Rafe has found the gun empty now. He throws it on the ground, grabs Lance, enraged, white-faced, barely in control.*)

RAFE: Don't you never...don't you never in your life...come around this camp again...with a loaded gun...

LANCE: Let go of me, don't fucking tell me - gimme back my gun-

RAFE: (*Shaking Lance violently.*) Don't you never...you hear me? You hear me? You hear me?

LANCE: (*Shocked and too drunk to fight.*) Okay, shit, let go... (*Rafe releases him, hurling him away. Lance staggers, almost falls, stares at Rafe. So does Jackie. Long moment as Rafe fights for*

control, then:)

RAFE: This is my place. Don't you *never*...(*Trails off, then.*) Get outa here...don't come back...till I ask ya. (*Lance looks at Rafe, disbelieving, then at Jakcie. Jackie looks away. Hurt and angry, turning away.*)

LANCE: Yeah, well...fuck you. And your sister too. (*Rafe jumps him - they go down - Rafe is savagely pummeling Lance as Jackie leaps on top of both of them and tries to pull Rafe off.*)

JACKIE: No, Rafe, Rafe, he's drunk, he can't fight, Rafe, come on, he don't mean it, he's drunk, come on...(*Jackie gets Rafe off Lance - they roll away, Rafe trying to control himself. Lance lies motionless...then finally stirs, manages to sit up. Jackie goes over and tries to help Lance up. Lance shoves him away, shakily gets to his feet, picks up his gun, almost falling over, looks at Rafe.*)

LANCE: Some fucking friend.

RAFE:...Not no more.

LANCE:(*Shaken, but:*)...Fine by me. Fucking head case. (*Starts out*)

RAFE: I got a gun too, Lance. You come up here again with a loaded gun, I'll shoot ya.

LANCE: (*Stops, looks at him.*) You're *alone*, asshole. Ask Jackie. You're *alone*. (*Goes out.*)

Crossfade. Others exit as Lance puts on the Dad mask, sits in a cheap folding lawn chair. Beer in one hand, shot glass of whiskey in the other, he addresses the audience.

DAD: I'll just say one thing and then I'll shut up. There are some folks in this world, if they wake up in the morning and they can see dollar signs, it's a good day. And if they can't, it ain't. (*Dad drains the shot. Lights up on Dylan and Ruby, jackets over their jeans, sitting on a blanket in the woods, wrapped up in each other. Beat of silence; then:*)

RUBY: You can smell the winter coming out here in the woods.

DYLAN:...Yeah.

DAD: Now you take Rafe and Evan Brooks...there's a pair to draw to.

RUBY: You know I'm restless.

DYLAN:...Yeah.

DAD: Them two were at loggerheads, and they were bound to be. Cause when it come to dollar signs, them two were night and day.

RUBY: Well, ain't it time?

DYLAN:...We got it pretty good here.

RUBY: (*Moves to look at him.*) What's good about it? (*Beat; hoping to avoid a fight, Dylan cuddles her back into the same position. Meanwhile, Dad goes on:*)

DAD: But, you know, at basics, them two were the same. Neither of 'em could sit still, put their feet up, have a drink - leave it for a while. Hell, no. One of 'em was busy doing nothing, and the other one was busy doing nothing yet.

DYLAN: The thing is, Brooks...he's got a lot to offer, there...

RUBY: You mean *here*?

DYLAN:...Well...

RUBY: I'm ready for something! Can't you feel that? (*Dylan hesitates, trying to find the way to handle this. He goes to kiss her - she moves away impatiently as:*)

DAD: Rafe, now...he was out there every day, sun up to sun down, with them draft horses, training 'em to do the chores like in Granddad's day. He took and bought a sawmill, one of them that's movable, you sit it in a wagon or a flatbed truck and bring the sawmill to the logs. I seen him hauling it with his team and wagon, hauling it right down the two-lane highway that's the onliest main road from here to anywhere, and stuck behind him was a whole long train of trucks and high-wheelers and them fancy rice-burners and macaroni-burners and krautmobiles them city folks like to drive up here. (*With some pride.*) And do you think that boy would turn out, let them folks go by? (*Laughs.*) Hell, no! He was holding up the whole parade and he liked it that way! Now Brooks would do that too with them two, they *are* the parade.

DYLAN: Listen, Ruby. We gotta wait, we gotta play this out. See, Brooks...he's got a lotta money. All these investments, properties, he's partners in all kinds of things - your family's land is nothing compared to what he's got. (*Ruby stares as Dad goes on:*)

DAD: But here's the difference, and you listen to what I'm telling ya. Every day's a good day for Brooks, cause all's he sees is dollar signs every blessed day.

RUBY: How do you know that?

DYLAN:...I found out some things.

DAD: But Rafe...you could put them dollar signs in his food, he'd spit 'em out and rinse his mouth out...just his way. (*Calls offstage:*) Ceelie, come on out here now and bring that whiskey! (*Mom enters with the whiskey bottle, moves slowly to Dad. Lights dim on them, leaving them in silhouette, Mom standing motionless behind Dad's chair. Meanwhile Ruby goes on:*)

RUBY: But we don't need his money if we get outa here! What about all them places you told me about?...that town in Mexico with the old hotel...and the birds...did you just make that up?

DYLAN: No...

RUBY: Where the birds in winter...

DYLAN:...the migrating birds in winter...

RUBY:...when they come to fly through this little town in Mexico...

DYLAN:...the old hotel is in their path...the big old hotel in the square...and they fly through the open windows...

RUBY:...this stream of birds with beating wings...

DYLAN: ...and out the other side again...

RUBY: I want to be there! If we go now, maybe we could see them -

DYLAN: Ruby, Brooks has so much money - and he likes us, he could change everything for us -

RUBY:(*Betrayed.*) You said the next place was your favorite place!

DYLAN: Ruby, listen...I'm so tired of hitchhiking. It's so much work, talking to the people...letting them think you're anybody they want you to be. I'm sick of starting over...begging for jobs that turn my stomach...sleeping anywhere a stranger'll let me have a couch, a floor -

RUBY: A bed?

DYLAN: ...A real bed?...Yeah.

RUBY: I would never do that with somebody I didn't love.

DYLAN:(*Simply.*) You don't know what you'll do. But now I can't go back to that. I love it here. It's beautiful...it's clean. I love living in this old house, like I'm part of the family that built it and took care of it and filled it for so many years -

RUBY:(*Bewildered.*) But that's my family -

DYLAN: No. They don't live here anymore. Brooks doesn't live here. I live here! And you can too - if I just give Brooks what he wants -

RUBY: I won't be beholden to Brooks or nobody! He can ask *me* for favors, I ain't asking him!

DYLAN: Ruby, please, don't mess this up for me -

RUBY:(*A cry:*) You can't change now - I love you! (*They embrace.*)

Mary Gallagher

Lights dim to silhouette Ruby and Dylan as well as Mom and Dad..
A single spotlight on Rafe as he addresses the audience.

RAFE: When you go inside the gate, they lock the gate behind you.
And when you go inside a door, they lock the door behind you.
Pretty soon you're locked so far inside, it's like being underground.
And you can't get out. You think about the air a lot. Feels like there
ain't enough. Thousands of men inside them walls, and it's all sealed
up. Locked windows with bars on 'em, and all them tight-locked
doors. And the ceiling's pressing down on you, like you're miles
down underground. Feels like it's hard to breathe. When your shift's
over, they let you free for that little while. But the whole time you're
outside, sucking in the clean air and looking at the sky, you got this
tightness in your chest and this pressure above your eyes like
something pressing down on you, cause you gotta go back. You
don't wanta go to sleep, cause that'll bring the time closer when
you'll walk through them gates again. And you do, you got to.
Every time you hear them locks start to turn behind you, you want to
scream out something and hurl them doors open and run. But you
can't. You're in there, you're living in there, like the cons. Only
difference is, they know when they're getting out. Cause you gotta
stay in there long enough to buy your land...and ain't no way of
knowing yet how long that'll be. (*Light spot moves to Dad. He
raises his full shot glass.*)

DAD: Here's to all you lovely people. "As good as you are, I'm as
bad as I am. And as bad as I am, I'm as good as you are." (*Dad
tosses off the shot as Lights up full on the group. A Sunday
gathering: Dad, Mom,Rafe,Julie, Ruby, Dylan. Everyone gets
drinks, beer for the others, Coke for Rafe. Dad looks at Rafe.*) Come
on now, I hardly ever see ya, have a real drink, for Chrissakes.

RAFE: I'll stick with this.

MOM:(*To Dad:*) You told me to have him over, don't get *at* him -

*They embrace. Lights dim to silhouette. Ruby and Dylan as well as
Mom and Dad. A single Spotlight on Rafe as he addresses the
audience.*

DAD:(*Mildly:*) Aw, hush up, woman. (*To Rafe:*) Your ma tells me
you're working at the prison now.

RAFE: That's right.

DAD: Well, that's a man's job, I respect that.

RAFE: I don't. I'm doing it because I got to.

DAD: Well, that's what I'm saying.

RAFE: Gotta have a steady job to get a mortgage. (*Pause.*)

DAD: What the hell you doing now?

RAFE: I ain't changed.

DAD: Boy...are you telling me you're gonna pay a bloodsucker's interest on land that this family owned free and clear six months ago?

RAFE: If that's what it takes.

DAD: You just ain't gonna face it that that land is lost to you.

RAFE: It ain't until I say it is.

DAD: (*Stares at him, then:*) You...you are the orneriest, pigheadedest, dug-in-deepest son of a bitch that I ever heard of.

RAFE: Prob'ly so.

DAD: (*Beat; then:*) Well, good for you, boy! You want it, you go after it!

RAFE: That's what I'm doing. (*Dad smiles at Rafe. Rafe looks at him stonily: no forgiveness. Mom has been covertly watching Dylan. Now she speaks, surprising herself and the others.*)

MOM: Dylan, you like that pie? There's more.

DYLAN: Oh, no, thanks - it was great, though, yeah -

DAD: (*Cutting through this:*) Where you from, boy?

DYLAN: ...No place special.

DAD: Where's your kinfolks?

DYLAN: ...Spread around.

DAD: Don't see 'em?

DYLAN: No, sir.

DAD: So you don't call no place home?

DYLAN: This is home for now.

RUBY: We're gonna travel.

DAD: Oh you are. Using what for money? (*Beat; all the others note this as Ruby gives Dad a charming, direct look.*)

RUBY: We gotta talk about that private.

DAD: Oh you say so, do you? (*Beat; then he slaps his leg.*) Come on over here and sit on your old man's lap. (*Rafe: and Julie can hardly believe the implications of this "private talk" as Ruby picks up the whiskey bottle and sits on her father's lap, filling his shot glass. Mom drifts over to take Ruby's place close to Dylan. Dylan is watching Ruby, doesn't notice Mom. To Dylan:*) What you got to offer, boy?

DYLAN: I'm a hard worker, sir.

DAD: Rafe here is the hardest goddamn worker in the county. What's it got him?

RAFE: I can stand to look in the mirror every morning.

DAD: Well, that's a cheap thrill. (*To Dylan:*) Rafe here is my boy, and pigheaded as he is, I stand by him because he's mine. But I never made nothing easy for him in his life, no more'n my dad did for me.

DYLAN: I'm not asking for help from you.

DAD: Well, good. Then who is? (*Brooks enters, hesitant at seeing Rafe, Julie and Dylan. Everyone's surprised, suddenly more formal - Ruby jumps up, Dad rises.*)Well, looky here! Come on in, neighbor -

BROOKS: Hello, everybody - didn't know I was interrupting a party -

DAD: - Ruby, get a beer for Mr. Brooks - or would you have a *real* drink with me?

BROOKS: (*To Dad and Ruby:*) Call me Evan, please - I can't stay, I (*Takes beer from Ruby.*) - I'm not much for drinking -

DAD: Beer ain't drinking, Evan. Had your supper yet?

BROOKS: Uh...well...enough that...really, I just had an impulse...I'm driving back to the city in about an hour, and I wondered if Ruby...(*Looks at Ruby, then at Mom and Dad.*)...if you wouldn't mind if Ruby came along for a visit. (*Dead silent pause. Everyone looks at Ruby, who struggles to seem nonchalant. Mom is now very close to Dylan, murmurs in his ear so only he hears it:*)

MOM: You see?

DAD: (*Speechless for once. Finally:*)...What...you mean...what?

BROOKS: Ruby was telling me a while back that she'd like to see the city. And I have a big place, guest rooms and all that, comforts of home, you know. I thought you might feel safer with somebody you know looking after her.

DAD: (*Instantly.*) Oh, no question. (*Beat; trying to assess this, thrown.*) Well...Ruby...? (*Ruby won't look at Dylan, who's willing her to say no. All the others wait: high drama which she loves. Suddenly she smiles at Brooks.*)

RUBY: Well, I *am* restless...

DYLAN: (*Can't help himself.*) What about your job?

DAD: Oh, we'll take care of that.

Mary Gallagher

BROOKS: Well, fine, then I'll swing by for you in about an hour...(*Beat as he smiles at her, then catches himself; to Dad:*) Thanks for the beer. (*To Mom as he goes:*) Bye-bye... (*Brooks goes out. They all look after him politely, waiting in silence till he's out of earshot. Ruby breaks this, starts out, passing Dad:*)

RUBY: Well, I better figure out what clothes to take - (*Dad grabs Ruby by her clothes and holds her, as she starts to laugh, swats at him. He's beaming proudly.*)

DAD: Private talks, eh? - *guess* you've been having some private talks. (*To Dylan:*) You better have another beer, son. Ain't no keeping up with her. (*Dylan jumps up and bolts out, Mom and Ruby watching him. Ruby's scared but too stubborn to follow him - she's going to make her point at whatever cost.*)

RUBY: (*To Dad and others:*)...I'm not changing. I'm just making sure.

DAD: Listen. My girl deserves the best. Didn't I always say so?

RUBY:...I'll get the best. But it might not be what you think.

DAD: Be smart now. Don't get pigheaded like your brother. If you really got a chance...you're a smart girl. *Be* smart. (*Ruby looks at Mom. Mom drops her eyes to hide her excitement, gives a little who knows? gesture. Ruby looks at Rafe.*)

RAFE:(*Simply.*) He could change everything for me.

RUBY:(*Beat; then, somewhat overwhelmed:*) We don't even know what he wants yet.

DAD:(*Slaps her on the butt.*) Well, go find out, girl! (*Ruby looks at Dad a beat, then laughs, trying for bravado, and exits. Dad: and Mom exit too as Light narrows down to Rafe and Julie.*)

JULIE: She's gonna get it all, ain't she? I'd like to kill her.

RAFE: Easy now.

JULIE: You're crazy if you think she'll help you.

107

RAFE: She don't need to help me much - just not get in my way.

JULIE: Rafe...are you gonna get yourself a real place to live or not? You got a good job now -

RAFE: I'm gonna stay right where I am as long as I can. It's rugged. But the more money I save, Julie, the quicker I can buy that land.

JULIE: The meadow.

RAFE: Yeah, the meadow...and after that maybe -

JULIE: "After that?" He wants a hundred thousand for that pukey little meadow! How much is he gonna want for the house? Or the long field? Or the orchard -

RAFE: I can't worry about that now -

JULIE: Rafe, for a hundred thousand dollars, right here in this county, you could buy a working farm, with a house and a barn and maybe fifty acres - maybe more -

RAFE: I don't want them farms. This is my land. I'm meant to have it, Julie. You gotta back me up on this. We'll...we'll work things out about us...

JULIE: I give up, Rafe.

RAFE: ...Don't give up...

JULIE: I am. Don't come around. I mean it.

RAFE:(*Beat; then:*) Up to you. I'll miss you. (*Julie slaps him hard. He stares, amazed, then grabs her arm, anger flying up.*) Don't you never do that again.

JULIE: No, I won't. I won't care enough. (*She exits, Rafe watching her*).

Crossfade to Rafe's camp. Night. Rafe sits reassembling his rifle after cleaning it. He addresses the audience:

Mary Gallagher

RAFE: First time my dad took me hunting, we came up here to camp, the two of us, and we took our guns and went deep into the woods and sat on a big rock, holding our guns, and ready. And we sat. Seemed like hours. Dad didn't move a muscle, so I didn't either. Got real hungry, had to piss bad - but I didn't move. Then I seen her, a big, pretty doe coming toward us maybe thirty yards away, coming through the brush and walking straight at us, with that almost floating look they got on them twiggy legs, but you can see the strength in 'em too...Dad, he didn't move. And then I seen another doe behind her, and another...coming toward us in a line, like they was bewitched, like we'd called 'em to us. But Dad still didn't move. I was getting wild inside, sweating through my clothes - wild to get a clear shot while I could, while I had at least a chance of getting my first deer, showing Dad what I could do. But he was so still, I couldn't even feel his breathing, up close against him like I was, and I couldn't do nothing but what he would do...till there was thirteen doe coming toward us, and the closest one I swear was gonna come right up to me and nuzzle me for sugar...and Dad still didn't move. And then he moved so quick, I hadn't hardly felt him move 'fore I heard his gun crack out and seen that big buck fall - that big six-pointer coming at the end of the line of doe, like Dad knowed he would do. He got him. I seen him fall. Them doe were scattering everywhere, and we just watched 'em go, and I said, "You got him, Dad!" And my dad said, "Well, I did, didn't I?"...After that...I was wild to go hunting...hunting with my dad. (*Beat; Rafe hears footsteps in the brush, stands listening, gun ready. Another beat; then:*)

RAFE: (*Calls:*) Lance? (*Rafe fires a warning shot into the air: BLAM!*)

DYLAN: (*Offstage.*) Hey, it's Dylan!

RAFE: (*Beat; then:*) Come ahead. (*Lowers the gun. Dylan enters. He carries a much-used duffel bag which is mostly empty. He's in a somewhat shaky state these days, and the shot didn't help. He stops, looks at Rafe and the gun.*) Had some problems. Now I'm careful.

DYLAN:...Sure.

RAFE: (*Beat; then:*) Surprised you could find the trail.

DYLAN: Ruby showed me where it was.

RAFE: She back?

DYLAN: No...no...before, I mean...she showed me before... (*Rafe nods. He doesn't ask, but Dylan sees that he wants to know, so:*) I haven't heard from her.

RAFE:...Huh. (*Beat; then:*) Want a Coke or something?

DYLAN: (*Long beat; then:*) Listen. (*Another long beat; then:*) I found something. (*Dylan squats, opens the duffel bag, takes out a cardboard box. Rafe sits, watches as he lays the gun down. Dylan holds the box for a beat, then hands it out toward Rafe. Rafe looks at Dylan, who seems so odd and shaky, then takes the box, sets it down carefully. He opens it, looks in for a long beat. He looks at Dylan, then lifts from the box some bones, holds them up in the firelight, staring. He looks at Dylan.*)

DYLAN: I was digging...planting trees. Between the farmhouse and the road. (*Another silence as Rafe examines the bones. Then:*)

RAFE: Don't look like any animal bones I've seen. (*Looks at Dylan*) You found 'em by the farmhouse?

DYLAN:(*Nods, then:*) It's your family's land. I thought...

RAFE: You brung 'em to me. That was right. (*Rafe puts the bones gently back into the box. He's somewhat shaken, but trying not to show it. He closes the box, looks at Dylan.*) No way of telling who it is or how they got there.

DYLAN: ...No way we can tell.

RAFE: ...I'll bury 'em up here. (*Dylan nods mutely. Rafe holds his gaze a beat, then:*) Preciate it. (*Rises.*) I'll get the shovel.

DYLAN:(*Rises, blurts*) I need help from you. (*Rafe turns, wary, expressionless, looks at Dylan. Then:*)

RAFE: I can't side with you.

Mary Gallagher

DYLAN: He'll never give you what you want.

RAFE: It ain't a gift - I'm working for it -

DYLAN: He doesn't care. About *her*, either.

RAFE: We don't know that yet. (*Beat; then, gently:*) You don't gotta get caught in this. I'd move on if I was you. (*Rafe exits to get the shovel. Dylan watches, motionless for a long beat. Then he grabs Rafe's gun, runs out.*)

Crossfade to Mom at night, outside their house. She stands looking out, thinking of Dylan alone at the farmhouse. Dad, played by Lance, emerges from the shadows.

DAD: Ceelie? Come on to bed now. (*Mom doesn't move or answer. Dad touches her. She jumps.*) Come on, girl.

MOM: I'll sit up for a while. (*Dad hesitates, rubs her back lightly. She doesn't respond.*)

DAD: You waiting up for Ruby?

MOM: (*Beat; then:*) I'm gonna walk a little in the moonlight. (*Mom exits, Dad watching her.*)

DAD: It's black dark out there.

Crossfade to the porch of the farmhouse. Dylan has Rafe's gun, sits in a porch chair, motionless, waiting. After a beat, Rafe enters, cautiously. Rafe can't see Dylan, but he can sense his presence - he stops, squats, ready to hit the ground if Dylan fires. Then:

RAFE: (*Very gently.*) Dylan? (*Dylan jumps convulsively. The gun jumps but doesn't fire. Bent low, Rafe moves, to make himself a tougher target, as he speaks again:*) Okay, now...I come to get my gun. (*Pause. No sound except their breathing. Then:*) It's my gun. I can't let you do like this. No harm done yet. Put a light on, let's sit down and talk about it. (*No answer. Faint light up on Mom inside the house area, listening, frightened for herself and Dylan. She can't see Dylan or the gun, only listens, very still. Finally:*) Okay, I'm gonna hafta go get help. I don't wanta do that. But I can't let you

111

have that gun. (*Rafe rises. Dylan raises the gun slowly and points it in Rafe's direction as Rafe walks away in a crooked route, trying not to give in to his fear. Dylan remains poised to shoot till Rafe is offstage. Then Mom speaks from the doorway.*)

MOM: I'm here. (*Dylan swings the gun in her direction, then drops it, very thrown and shaky, jumping up.*)

DYLAN: Ruby? (*Mom steps closer, into a patch of moonlight.*)

MOM: Ceelie. I'm here.

DYLAN: ...Is it Ruby? Did she send a message?

MOM: Don't you see how Ruby is? She won't never make it easy -

DYLAN: Is she coming back tonight?

MOM: She's with *him*. (*Brief pause.*)

DYLAN: What do you want? (*Mom touches his face very delicately. Dylan stares, then abruptly backs up a step, breaking contact.*) You better get outa here. I don't know what's gonna happen.

MOM: I got money hid from him. We can go away.

DYLAN:...I can't do that anymore...

MOM: Listen. When Ruby come along...some way he was lost to me. And I ain't never got him back. And now Ruby is lost to you -

DYLAN: Not till I say she is!

MOM: You can talk like them. But you and me, we ain't like them -

DYLAN: Quit talking now! Get outa here!

MOM: I don't want to watch them lay your body in the ground -

DYLAN: (*Points rifle at her.*) Get out! (*Mom goes.*)

Crossfade to the driveway outside Ruby's house. Ruby and Brooks walk slowly toward the house, as if both are a little reluctant to end this time together. Brooks carries Ruby's suitcase.

RUBY: I like your car.

BROOKS: You do, huh?...Not too many of those in your neck of the woods...Looks like your folks are out.

RUBY: More likely they're asleep.

BROOKS: Had a good time this week?

RUBY:(*Airy.*) Oh, I could live like that.

BROOKS:(*Amused, charmed.*) Think so? Takes money.

RUBY: You've got that part.

BROOKS:(*Laughs.*) Is this a proposal? (*Ruby gives a little ambiguous laugh. Brooks looks at her, Stops walking, somewhat awkwardly and shyly stops her too. She looks at him, giving nothing away.*)...You couldn't really picture that, could you?

RUBY: What?

BROOKS:...Well, you know...us as a couple. It's just too far-fetched.

RUBY: Why?

BROOKS: Well, it's pretty obvious...

RUBY: (*As if objective.*) You're not that much older.

BROOKS:...Old enough. And your family and mine combined, that's quite an image...but you're something, Ruby. Don't think I haven't...well. I've gotta be careful not to spend too much time around you. (*Beat; then he gives in, moves to kiss her. She stops him by saying coolly:*)

RUBY: I wouldn't give up Dylan for all your money. (*Brooks* *freezes, then pulls back, stung.*)

BROOKS: Really. I didn't see you as a romantic, Ruby. And I can't imagine Dylan will be able to keep you in the style you aspire to. Even with a second income from McDonald's.

RUBY: I won't care, with him. (*Beat; then:*) We're leaving anyway.

BROOKS: He hasn't told me.

RUBY: I just did.

BROOKS: (*Beat; then:*) I hurt your feelings when I said that about your family, didn't I? And again just now. I'm sorry -

RUBY: That's not why. (*Takes suitcase.*) I had a good time. Thanks. (*She swiftly kisses him, lingering just long enough to let him know what he's missing, and goes out. He stands watching her.*)

Crossfade to the farmhouse. Rafe and Dad, played by Lance, are approaching the farmhouse in the dark, both with rifles. Dad stops, says softly:

DAD: Rafe. (*As Rafe stops:*) After this, no more talking.

RAFE: (*Softly.*) Right.

DAD: (*Beat; then:*) Think he's waiting there for Brooks?

RAFE:...Maybe Brooks. Maybe not. (*Beat; then*) Maybe he won't hurt nobody -

DAD: We gotta make sure of that.

RAFE: You talk to him. Maybe he'll give the gun to you -

DAD: Maybe he'll shoot me, too. Don't pull back now. I ain't gonna shoot unless I got to, but I need you to follow my lead here. Will you do that?

RAFE:...Yeah.

Mary Gallagher

DAD: That's why you came and got me, ain't it? *(Rafe takes this as a deep cut, but says nothing. Long beat; then:)* Now stay pretty close. We don't wanta fan out too much, might shoot each other.

RAFE:...Right.

DAD: Wish it wasn't so goddamn dark. *(Turns head to listen.)* Car coming. Might be them, come on.

As Dad and Rafe start forward, quickly and quietly, Crossfade to Dylan in the farmhouse. He stands motionless, the rifle held loosely at his side. Through a window, headlights sweep across the porch area and house with sound of car arriving. Then lights and sound fade out. Dylan doesn't move, but every muscle is alert and listening.

Lights up on Ruby walking slowly through the meadow in the dark. She's coming to see Dylan, but taking her time, feeling very happy and powerful, and humming to herself the melody of "Mill o' Tifty's Annie." She looks up at the stars. Humming, she stops, stretches up as if to touch them: on top of the world. Her humming continues through the scene, but is not heard by the others.

Dylan speaks his thoughts aloud, words he's been going over and over in his head for days:

DYLAN: Mr. Brooks...I just want to ask you respectfully...see, Ruby and I...Ruby means more to me, and we...we don't have a place to go...and we belong here, Mr. Brooks...

BROOKS:*(Calls from darkness:)* Hey, Dylan! Put the porchlight on! *(Ruby's humming is the only sound as Dylan hesitates, then flicks an invisible switch: Light fills the porch area. Brooks is approaching the porch, carrying his overnight case, throws a hand up to shield his eyes for a moment. Lights up faintly on Dad and Rafe, crouched to fire.)*

DAD:*(Mutters to Rafe.)* That was his first mistake, right there.

RAFE:*(Trembling, aimed to fire.)* Maybe he won't do nothing, maybe he's just scared.

DYLAN:(*In doorway, partly seen.*) Mr. Brooks...where's Ruby?

BROOKS:(*As if amused.*) Well, you won, Dylan.

DYLAN: ...What? (*Sound of Ruby humming as she begins to dance beneath the stars. Dylan steps forward into the light. Brooks sees the gun dangling in Dylan's hand.*)

BROOKS: What's with the gun? (*Dylan looks at him, then starts to make a dazed explaining gesture that sweeps the rifle upward. In one convulsive move, Rafe fires. Dylan jerks backward violently and falls.*)

Blackout on all but Ruby, who keeps dancing and humming in the meadow. Over the humming, as a slow Crossfade begins on Ruby.

DAD'S VOICE: Well, for good or ill, you got him, son.

Long Beat; Crossfade down on Ruby And up on three masked figures: Dad: (Dylan,) Brooks: (Jackie,) and Mom: (Darlene.) They address the audience one by one:

DAD: Oh, I know I had a part in it. And I gotta carry that. And I will. I do. But you know, more than that, what I think is, that boy of Ruby's was disturbed...all twisted up inside, like a tree that's windshook. Sometimes you take and cut a hemlock down that looks beautiful, all big and straight and fine. But when you cut it open, it just falls apart. Cause it's been so twisted and wrenched around by these winds up here in these mountains that the grain can't hold together. The other trees can take it, but somehow a windshook tree...you take and cut it open, and it crumbles in your hands...

BROOKS: I wanted to call the sheriff or the state troopers - and to his credit, so did Rafe. But his father was convinced that to keep Rafe out of prison, we had to keep it to ourselves. And Rafe had saved my life...or meant to, anyway...so I went along. I think they must have buried him somewhere on the land...where he had been planting trees...well, after that, I couldn't even go there. So I put the house and land up for sale, and sold them. I thought Rafe would remind me of his offer to buy the meadow...and I would have felt compelled to sell it to him...probably...but I never heard from him. Strange people. (*Not true.*) I don't think about them.

Mary Gallagher

Mom removes her mask and becomes Darlene as Lights fade on the others.

DARLENE: I think I'm the only outside one who knows. Well, Ruby...she had to have someone to talk to...acting crazy like she was...I guess she knew I'd understand how it coulda happened, cause Dale and me...I hate to think it, specially cause of Ashley...but *we* could end up some way like that. Things happen. (*Beat; then:*) But then Ruby's dad give her some money, and she left. She sent me a postcard from some little town out west where they got folks dress up like cowboys and indians and sunbonnet ladies and act out scenes, you know. That was the picture on the postcard. I woulda like to seen that. Said she was on a Greyhound bus, on her way to Mexico. But after that, I didn't hear nothing. And Rafe...seemed like he just kept going. Working at the prison...tending to them big huge horses...Then come spring, he built a cabin up there on the mountain, somewheres around where their old hunting cabin used to be.

(*Fade to black.*)

THE END

REINDEER SOUP

by Joe Pintauro

ABOUT THE PLAYWRIGHT

Joe Pintauro is a company writer at New York's Circle Repertory Theatre. His recent stage plays include *Raft of the Medusa*, which opened at New York's Minetta Lane Theater in December 1991; and *Wild Blue*, a collection of eight short plays which premiered at New York's 47th Street Playhouse and was recently produced at San Francisco's Theatre Rhinoceros. *Snow Orchid* was his first full-length play and was a selection of the Eugene O'Neill Conference. *Beside Herself* was also produced at Circle Rep. *Cacciatore* (Hudson Guild and the Edinburgh Festival). He has written over thirty one-act plays, several of which have been presented in full-evening productions under the titles; *Wild Blue*, *Rules of Love*, *Cacciatore*, *On the Wing* and *Moving Targets*, and *Metropolitan Operas*. In addition, the National Theatre Institute has produced a number of these plays in Russian and English. Recently, Mr. Pintauro's adaptation of Peter Matthiessen's *Men's Lives* premiered at New York's new Bay Street Festival Theater. Mr. Pintauro has created three award-winning books of poetry, which were illustrated by Sister Mary Corita, and he is the author of short works of fiction and novels (*Cold Hands* and *State of Grace*).

Reindeer Soup was commissioned for and first presented by the Young Conservatory at American Conservatory Theater (Carey Perloff, Artistic Director, John Sullivan, Managing Director), San Francisco, California on August 21, 1992. The Director was Craig Slaight; Assistant to the Director was Jennifer Paige Butsch; the lighting was designed by Todd Guttmann; the sound was designed by Scott Robinson; and Norman was created by Cour Dain.

The cast was as follows:

CHARLIE .... Paul Shikany
POP .... Devon Angus
JULIE .... Adela Laczynski
KLUTE................................. Adam Costello
CHRISSIE .... .Sara Waldhorn
VINCE .... James Tucker
RADIO ANNOUNCER .... Joshua Costello
MOM................................. ... Courtney Fowler
IONA.................................. Dawnn Steeves
VOICE OF MELISSA .... : ...... Jennifer Paige Butsch

ABOUT THE PLAY

I met a friend on the street in New York City, a woman whom I hadn't seen in years. She was with her little daughter, a six year old.

"This is Bridget," The woman said.

"She looks just like you." I said. "She's a beautiful child."

I was shocked when my friend asked: "Won't you please address her? I'm sure she'd appreciate it." What had I done? I'd acted as though the child wasn't there! Was it because the child's face was far below me? Was it because I assumed children don't listen, that they are numb, that they are to be treated differently? Had this woman introduced me to an adult and had I acted the same it would have been a blatant rudeness. I offered my hand to the child and said, "Hello, I'm Joe. You look as beautiful as your mother today." "I'm Bridget. Thanks." The little girl said simply. It was a lesson I vowed never to forget.

When I was asked to write a play for children, my first instinct was to be careful that I didn't make the same mistake. Children don't deserve to be treated like diminished persons. They love deeply, feel passion, are haunted by loss, sometimes more

121

than adults. When an adult loses a mate, she or he may always find another. When a child loses a parent, that loss will be with the child till the end of her or his life.

I thought of *Reindeer Soup* first in terms of the values I wanted to put forward, values that surround dark and inscrutable things like death, poverty, hunger, parental loss and social and economic chaos. In my play, it is not Christmas, though one character who has lost track of time, believes it to be. The holiday, normally a time of giddiness and fantasy, is a misplaced event in my play, the reindeer, a cold and helpless victim of deliberate violence. The children are waiting not for Santa, but for salvation from a corrupt and failed society and yet, their dilemma is somehow bravely elevated, charged with mystery and expectation. In fact, *Reindeer Soup* is an adult play, written to include children. I remembered the lesson of Bridget and wrote in the same uncensored way that I would normally.

Children have a right to our intelligence, to our poetry and wisdom. Moreso than the rest of us, children are on a lonesome path, trying to make sense of this world. I hope *Reindeer Soup* throws a little light in the way of anyone on that path.

Joe Pintauro
September,1992
Sag Harbor

CHARACTERS

POP: Alternately sad and comedic. He has delusions of grandeur but is otherwise a good father. (45-50)

MOM: She is your typical good American mom, good-looking, selfless and energetic. (40-45)

VINCE: The oldest boy - handsome, strong, bright. (19)

CHARLIE: Mentally handicapped with learning disabilities, he is brave, eager and sincere. (17)

KLUTE: Dark and brooding, angry and grief-stricken. (14)

JULIE: Principalled, rebellious and intelligent. (12)

CHRISSIE: The youngest, is scared, dependent and a sweet, good child. (8)

IONA: She is ascetical, a being of mythic dimensions, some one wise who has seen the other side of life, (and death). Perhaps she's some kind of angel.

SETTING

We're in a large barnlike space - a snow cellar similar to a potato barn. There are bunks all around and a huge pot as big as a whale blubber pot on a monstrous woodburning stove that is so large it heats up the entire space. A galvanized garbage pail may be used. Downstage right, there is a sliding door that opens to a frozen wasteland. A blizzard is occurring. We hear its terrible music whenever the big sliding door is opened. This is the only door in the space.

Reindeer Soup

Pop is asleep tied up in a chair. All others except Vince and Charlie are in their bunks asleep. There's a loud bang on the door. Charlie slides it open. Vince stumbles in, throwing off his outer clothes.

CHARLIE: Vince? My God. You're all wet.

VINCE: I fell in a stream.

CHARLIE: You mean like...water? How? Everything's frozen out there.

VINCE: Well I fell into a stream and it was wet.

CHARLIE: But Vince. Are you kidding? The streams have been frozen since September.

VINCE: I'm wet. Feel me. Wet. Don't tell me I didn't fall into a stream.

CHARLIE: But a bucket of water outside freezes in two seconds.

VINCE: Feel this bread. Still wet. I traded a months pay at the company store at the gold mine and bought bread and beans and vegetables for Julie. The bags were so heavy I tried to short cut through the industrial area next to the pine forest and I came to this stream, I never said to myself, hey this stream can't be flowing in sub zero weather. I just took off my snowshoes and stepped on this stone but it was slimy and I slipped. A whole month's salary went downstream, 20 cans of tuna fish, bags of dried fruit, 30 lbs of beans, macaroni, barley, rice and cereal...they disappeared. The only thing I managed to fish out was this bread.

CHARLIE: Sure coulda used those beans in my soup. Well, get those clothes off. This bread'll dry out. You hang out near the stove.(*Wraps bread in net.*)

VINCE:(*Changing out of wet clothes.*) What's the tree doing in the house?

CHARLIE: Pop thought it was Christmas again last week.

VINCE: Where did he get the power saw to cut it down?

CHARLIE: He kept crashing into it with the pickup till it fell over, then he tied a chain to it and dragged it home.

VINCE: Smells Christmasy. Better late than never. What're you cookin'?

CHARLIE: Soup.

VINCE: What's the stock?

CHARLIE: Lake ice.

VINCE: C'mon Charlie. There's ice in that pot?

CHARLIE: I discovered that blocks of ice chopped out of the lake are infinitely tastier than melted snow. There's kind of a fish smell to it.

VINCE: Charlie. There's only lake ice in that pot?

CHARLIE: I lay this in for flavor. (*He pulls up a sling of cheese cloth containing a small sphere about the size of a cantaloupe.*)

VINCE: My God, what is that?

CHARLIE: A racoon head. Used it four times already. Julie'll eat your bread. She won't eat soup because it's a meat base. (*Charlie ladles out a bown of soup.*)

VINCE: Doesn't somebody tell her it's not so cool to be a vegetarian this far north of Detroit?

CHARLIE: She'll eat the bread.

VINCE: Yeah, if it dries.

CHARLIE: I'll hang it over the oven with your clothes. (*He hangs bread on a clothesline over the stove and throws a blanket to Vince.*) And you drink that, drink that.

VINCE: Charlie this just tastes like hot water.

CHARLIE: Try some pepper.

VINCE: That's a little better.

CHARLIE: Maybe some mustard?

VINCE: No, thanks. Not this time. (*Tastes.*) Mmmmm. Wonderful. (*Lying.*) I'll just let it cool off here for a minute...

CHARLIE: No. Drink it down. It'll warm you up.

VINCE: No. No. I, I...wanna savor every drop. Slow...

CHARLIE: Boy. Am I glad you're back. No one here appreciates my cooking like you do Vince. This may sound silly but I tried cooking the rocking chair. Don't laugh. It was before Pop ran over the racoon.

VINCE: No. Pop ran over that racoon?

CHARLIE: If an animal crosses the road, instead of hitting the brake, he floors the accelerator and whack! We got road pizza! Two weeks ago we had a mink in this soup, now there's just a few bones left at the bottom. I keep the old man tied up a lot because, look. We're down to his last five pills, but it's better than t.v. watchin' him sometimes. When the pill wears off he thinks he's somebody else. Today he's Richard Nixon. Yesterday he was Our Miss Brooks. Who was Miss Brooks anyway?

VINCE: Wait-wait-wait. You mean, Pop has started to hunt animals by running them over with the truck?

CHARLIE: Ain't he brilliant? He turned the truck into a weapon. I wrap the animal in cheese cloth so the fur won't get in the soup and I just throw the poor thing in the pot. I figure the hot water sterilizes them. It's food, right?

Joe Pintauro

VINCE: Charlie, Charlie look at me.

CHARLIE: What.

VINCE: You're denying something here. Look straight at me. In the eyes. Charlie...

CHARLIE: I'm lookin'.

VINCE: You're telling me you throw dead animals in this pot and you feed that shit to these kids? Charlie you tie up Pop and use lake ice to make soup that's just hot water with a tea bag full of road pizza?

CHARLIE: Yes...(*Falling apart.*) Julie has lost weight. Little Chrissie sleeps so as not to feel hungry. I'm afraid she won't wake up sometimes. I...I get weak in the morning. I fainted yesterday.

VINCE: You fainted? Are you okay?

CHARLIE: I was standing there...near the stove and the next thing I know my head was on the floor and I was looking up at Julie. I drink the soup but it passes right through me. Klute's the only one who seems healthy. He has a whale steak and a shark fin under his bed which he won't let me use. He steals from us. He just hoards objects to trade with the Eskimos. If I didn't make that soup, they'd all die except Klute. Pop's condition is worse than ever. He hallucinates. There's only five of his pills left. Sometimes I worry that I've inherited his craziness.

VINCE: Shut up. There's nothing genetically wrong with you, him or us. Getting fired and having your wife crash the car head on...and driving north to find a cheaper life is a nightmare that would drive any man crazy. There's a huge hole in his life.

CHARLIE: Why didn't he take his hole down south where we could survive on coconuts at the public beach or scrounge grapefruits from the next door neighbors but he came north into Canada so far up? What for? People from Detroit are used to the cold but we don't know beans about the tundra. This is Eskimo country. You need fur coats and reindeer to get anywhere and you have to know how to fish in the ice and shoot caribou.

VINCE: Yeah, but this place was cheap.

CHARLIE: He went out and bought a new pick-up didn't he?

VINCE: So he could get work.

CHARLIE: Well where's the work? Of course houses are dirt cheap up here. There's no businesses, no markets, 'cept the Eskimos working in that funky old chemical plant and the gold mine. The truck's nice and black and shiny but far as we're concerned its just a stupid kitchen utensil for pounding out road meat and the needle is almost on empty anyway. It's a nightmare. When I fall asleep, I dream I've got a beautiful pot of soup here. We're in Detroit, the radio's playing in the kitchen and mom's making breakfast. When I wake up I have to face an empty pot full of hot lake water and a looney tunes father who thinks he is an ex-president of the United States. Did you know he packed Mom's clothes. On Sunday, he put on her old bathing suit and we had to tackle him because he was going out into the blizzard in her bathing cap.

VINCE: We've got to find the kids something to eat. I can't listen to this.

CHARLIE: Tell me about it. Julie's been waiting for her vegetables. What are you going to tell her?

VINCE: That I fell in a stream and the stuff went downstream.

CHARLIE: We didn't need that to happen Vince. I can't believe you did that.

VINCE: You cooked a rocking chair.

CHARLIE: I was staring at the rocking chair which was all apart in a heap anyway and I figured: Wood is a vegetable. The ice water was boiling with nothing to cook in it so I stuck the arm of the chair in the pot and let it boil for a day, but the shellack gave it a bitter taste...

VINCE: (*Sarcastic.*) You should've used the pine tree.

CHARLIE: I tried it. It tasted like cough-drops and it cleared our sinuses but it made little Chrissie sick.

VINCE: No. Don't feed this stupid stuff to them.

CHARLIE: Since the old man thinks he's our Miss Brooks no one in this house has had even a road pizza soup to eat. He can't go road hunting while he's tied up. So we all go hungry. We're starving. All we do all day is sleep... You get fed by the people at the mines.

VINCE: Where are your shoes?

CHARLIE: Klute stole 'em.

VINCE: Well take them back.

CHARLIE: Julie and I agreed to let him take anything he wants from us so that it won't be stealing. That's what Mom'd do. So he's in possession of my sneakers, but he didn't steal them technically.

VINCE: Charlie! He's a thief?

CHARLIE: No, no, no. I said to him Klute, everything in this house is yours, so you can have it and therefore you won't be a criminal, and he's been just takin' everything and hoarding it under his bunk and I think it's all because he really misses mom.

VINCE: But he should *know* he's a thief. How will he learn?

CHARLIE: Well I disagree with you. No brother of mine is going to be a thief, not if I can help it.

VINCE: But Charlie, he already is athief.

CHARLIE: Mom would die.

VINCE: Mom did die Charlie.

CHARLIE: Okay. Don't remind me of it. Okay?

VINCE: You need a rest Charlie. Do you have Pop's prescription for his pills?

CHARLIE: What good is it? There's no drug store for seventy-five miles and there's no money even if there was one next door. (*Gives Vince the prescription.*) Here. (*Pop comes toward audience, tied with rope, he falls.*)

POP: Who did this? Take these off me.

CHARLIE: No Vince. Pop? Pop? Hi. It's...guess who? Me?

POP: What?

VINCE: Me too, Pop. Vince.

POP: Vince who?

VINCE: I'm your number one son, you know. I work in the gold mine up a ways from here.

POP: You're shining.

VINCE: Shining? Me?

POP: Yes. You're some angel. No you're a ghost!

VINCE: Dad I'm not shining. I'm just a little damp cause I...never mind... You look not too bad at all.

POP: (*Points to a member of the audience.*) It's not my fault sir...I'm completely innocent.

VINCE: There's no shame in being fired.

POP: I was more than competent, they'll rue my absence. Look at things the way they are now.

VINCE: Pop, you were the foreman on the assembly line.

POP: What assembly line?

Joe Pintauro

VINCE: At G.M. pop. You made, cars, trucks...

POP: The C.E.O. Uh, he's Italian. Sounds like Coca Cola.

VINCE: Lee Iacocca?

POP: That's the man. (*To audience.*) He offered me a custom car and I refused it. No favors to industry and yet I get blamed for Cambodia, Kent State and Chile. I never sold arms to America's enemies. I didn't keep hostages from being freed or gave the banks carte blanche to suck the nation dry. No sir. But did they fire Reagan? No. They fired me and your mother had a stroke... (*Vince gets pills, Charlie a bowl of soup.*)

VINCE: No, no, no...there was a terrible accident.

CHARLIE: Head on collision.

VINCE: Pop, take one of these nice pills with some of Charlie's soup. Lee Iacocca never gave you anything.

POP: What's wrong with this boy?

VINCE: He fired you from General Motors this past July and you sold the house and bought a pick-up truck with your severance pay. You piled us in and we went north crossed the Makinaw bridge, way into Canada...and kept driving until we saw snow. Then winter came and we got stuck up here.. You swore you'd never throw away money on rent again. Remember that?

POP: Was your mother's name Beatrice?

VINCE: Yeah. Beattie. Hey Pop. Those pills work. So Pop we got this here barn cheap. Then you went out to find work with the pick-up and there were no jobs because basically, there was no town up here. Just caribou and wolves and the Eskimos come down from Baffin Island for the winter. All of a sudden Pop, November hit. Bam! We were trapped up here.

POP: Get hold of my wallet, Vince. We'll gas up the pick-up and go right back home.

VINCE: But Pop, the house in Detroit is sold. It's gone.

POP: My white roses? Let's drive down to Louisiana or Florida, we should have tried that first.

VINCE: Pop, it's going to take time now to save up that kind of money. One months wages at the mine and all I get is enough to keep us alive for a week, and I just lost all our months supplies because I fell into a damn stream. If we can just get through this winter, it'll be easier up here in the summer. Charlie'll be old enough for the mines and we can afford to buy you a steady supply of your medicine and then we can get out of here before next winter sets in.

POP: No, no, I can't give up Charlie.

CHARLIE: Pop. You gotta have hope.

POP: That's a hard word to visualize son.

VINCE: We know.

POP: I remember the word though.

VINCE: That's a start.

POP: Hope was a cheerleader in my high school. She wouldn't give me the time of day.

VINCE: Now Dad! This here's Charlie, your next to oldest. Right?

CHARLIE: Hi Pop.

POP: What's the matter with you? Don't you think I know my own kids?

VINCE: And Julie's over there. And little Chrissie is up there.

POP: Where's Vince?

VINCE: Huh? Pop, that's me.

POP: Who's that?

VINCE: Oh, that's Klute.

POP: He back? Oh...Charlie, why are you always tying me up son? Vince, get these ropes off me.

VINCE: Sure-sure Pop. (*He unties his father.*)

CHRISSIE: (*Sleepily, coming to Charlie.*) Charlie, when are we going home?

POP: She's dreaming again. Chrissie. Come here to Pop.

VINCE: Hey Chrissie, look up there, see that round thing? I got you that nice big round loaf of bread to eat when it dries.

CHRISSIE: Why is it wet?

POP: Now wait a minute...I'll be darned if that bread isn't shining.

VINCE: Huh? Shining?

POP: You too. I'm telling you, you're shining.

CHARLIE: Come to think of it, there's a lot of light around you Vince, can't you see it?

KLUTE: (*Sitting up in bed.*) Heh! Will you guys shut up and let me sleep for cryin' out loud.

VINCE: (*Goes to Klute's bed.*) Now that you're awake Klute, how about lending Charlie his own sneakers so he could warm his feet, I mean you've got four pair there. What do you need four pair for?

KLUTE: Go to hell. I need them. Cause they're mine, Vince. Bug off!

VINCE: Just lend them to him.

KLUTE: You don't understand Vince, so why don't you just hang it up? We were all doin' fine before you came.

VINCE: Fine? You got a tree on its side here and a big pot of nothing boiling away with a racoon head in it. Pop and Chrissie and Charlie look pretty pasty to me. How come you got rosey cheeks Klute?

KLUTE: Cause I go out.

VINCE: You got a little supply store under your bed?

KLUTE: Who died and left you boss Vince?

JULIE: He sneaks out and trades things with the Eskimos for food. He has a shark fin under his bed and whale steaks.

POP: No. Klute, you have food, son?

JULIE: Suppose that whale was a mother? What are her children going to do for milk? (*Vince goes to Klute's bed and looks under it.*)

KLUTE: It was a male whale.

JULIE: How would you know?

KLUTE: Get away from there you. Give me that...

VINCE: One can of Progresso Chicarina Chicken soup.

KLUTE: Gimme that.

VINCE: Dried papaya, prunes...a shark fin.

KLUTE: (*Struggling to regain his things.*) I'll kill you Vince.

VINCE: A can of pinto beans. Tuna fish. Don't touch me Klute or I'll knock you on your ass. Some kinda dried meat. Crackers. Soda. I don't see your sneakers Charlie.

JULIE: He traded them.

POP: Give Julie that dry papaya now.

KLUTE: No, let her eat Charlie's soup.

CHRISSIE: I've got the tuna and the papaya.

POP: *Bring* all that food to me.

VINCE: No please Pop. Chrissie. Julie, let Klute keep his food. Maybe Klute will change his mind. Let's give him an hour.

KLUTE: I'm not changing my mind so do whatever you have to do to get what you want. Kill me in my sleep, Vince. Here stab me. (*Holds out hunting knife to Vince.*)

Vince puts Chrissie to sleep. Charlie, sits with his head in his hands. Pop tucks Julie in and Vince kisses her goodnight. Klute hugs all his possessions, his sneakers, food and other objects, to his body and pulls the covers over him and the goods.

CHARLIE: (*Puts on his coat and snow shoes during the following, grabs ice tongs and throws a coat and hat at Vince.*) Hey Vince help me chop out some more lake ice for the pot.

VINCE: What's wrong with snow? We got mountains at our front door.

CHARLIE: You want my soup base to taste like acid rain?

VINCE: Charlie, this isn't Detroit, and it's snowing forever out there.

CHARLIE: So acid snow, make a liar out of me. Stay cool gang. We'll be goin' out into the stoooorrrrrmmmmm. (*The door slides open revealing the tumultuous blizzard outside. Charlie and Vince venture out.*)

POP: Cover up kids. (*Pop puts wood in stove.*)

JULIE: Tuck me in. (*He does.*) I miss you when you're not our Pop.

POP: Well the pill's working and I'm your Pop now so let's make sure you're warm enough.

JULIE: I would love it if somebody explained to me why you need a pill just to be a normal father.

POP:(*Thinks.*) The chemicals in my brain get messed up and I go flyin' off the track...(*He leaves her to go to table. She follows him.*)

JULIE: What track?

POP: My track. The track of who I am.

JULIE: When you have to be tied up, it's like not only Mom is gone but you are too.

POP: I feel very foolish but I didn't ask to be this way.

JULIE: I'm too young to be the mother around here...

POP: Oh yes. You're too young. You stay the twelve year old. Julie, that's exactly what your Mom would want. You're still a child. Pop'll take care of you and protect you.

JULIE: Do you have enough pills for that?

POP: Well...just remember you don't have to be grown up before your time. Now do Pop a favor and try to eat some of the things we do.

JULIE: That stupid soup is just filthy hot water.

POP: It has some nourishment now.

JULIE: Road pizza. I'd rather die.

POP: Where am I going to get vegetables in this wasteland up here?

JULIE: Why didn't you think of that six months ago? You're a horrible man. Eating meat is murder.

POP: That's nonsense.

JULIE: Obviously you feel that way since you're the one who kills the animals .

POP: Now I am not a murderer...

JULIE: Animals have a right to live you know. They survive out there through thick and thin. They have their babies in the snow. Oh, if we were out there we'd grow hair too. They're just like us. They're friends under that fur—and they mind their own business. What do they ask from us? Nothing. Nothing. They don't even want our help and we kill them...

POP: We kill vegetables when we eat them.

JULIE: Huh?

POP: I've heard carrots' scream. Yeah, and string beans and broccoli weeping.

JULIE:(*Hands over ears.*) I wasn't meant for this world. I'm wasting away, worrying about the elephants getting shot by poachers so some narcisstic bimbo could wear an ivory bracelet. I go to sleep each night wondering: how does that poor elephant feel? She's got her trunk up in the trees grabbing fruit for her baby and BAMMMMM! Mother is hit. Mother is dizzy. Run my darling child. Mother is falling to her knees. Oh the pain. I'm bleeding to death. Goodbye tree, goodbye clouds, BOOOOOM! I've fallen in a heap. My eyes are glaring—my trunk is swinging wildly. Oh no. They're coming closer. They're going to shoot again. The gun is touching my skull. BAMMMMM! In the brain. Goodbye light! The last thing I see is the giraffes running. The eagles soar up and away. They look down and see the cities covered in pollution...where will we go? The condors too. They swear to the god of all flying creatures they will never lay their eggs again. And how many people eat chickens each day? Twenty million? A hundred million? All those chickens murdered each day. All that blood all over the world. I think I'm going to faint. And now you tell me that stringbeans and broccoli feel it too. I just won't stand for it another minute. I'd rather...I'd rather...

POP: Shhh.

JULIE: Why didn't God make us so we didn't have to eat?

POP: If people didn't have to eat, they wouldn't work.

JULIE: Why did God make it so adults have to work, work, work. What are we slaves?

POP: No people want houses and fancy cars and boats and...

JULIE: Why aren't all those things free?

POP: You know, work, work is good.

JULIE: Yeah.

POP: Work can make you happy. Work is what you do with other people.

JULIE: I feel sorry for that poor whale and shark under Klute's bed. There's death in this house.

POP: Now that's not true.

JULIE: It reminds me of what happened to Mom and I get scared.

POP: But Julie, if you don't eat something...you might...you might even...

JULIE: Pop, wake up. We're starving here. We won't have food for another month. You made us be trapped up here with a beautiful truck that has a teeny bit of gas left and one continuous blizzard outside. No other kids, just Eskimos and reindeer. Pop, we're going to die.

POP: If you go to sleep, I'll think of something. How's that?

JULIE: Don't strain yourself. (*She goes back to bed.*)

POP: Maybe I could...maybe I could....(*Trying to get out of it, he goes to Chrissie's bunk.*) tuck in Chrissie. Hi, Angel.

Joe Pintauro

CHRISSIE: When is my mother coming back?

POP: You're who? Oh, well, hm...it's the rules of heaven that once you go in you can't come out.

CHRISSIE: Don't tell me God keeps people prisoner there, that's absurd.

KLUTE: The kid is smarter then you Pop.

POP: People in heaven are so happy, they just can't bring themselves to leave.

KLUTE: Don't believe him.

CHRISSIE: Mom wouldn't stay. She would look down at what we're going through and she'd come get us.

POP: Then you tell me where she is...you tell me.

KLUTE: She's dead, she's dead.

POP: She may, glimpse...she may, you know, glimpse what's goin' on here and she's stayin' up there...Because she figures we ain't all that bad off down here—things are pretty good.

KLUTE: I don't know if you're worse when you think you're Our Miss Brooks or when you think you're the Pope.

CHRISSIE: I know. Mom up in heaven figures, the sooner we die the quicker we'll be able to join her in heaven and Mom made Vince fall in the stream.

POP: Now just forget about your mother. Klute is right. We said goodbye to her. And she's gone from us. Now Klute, I'll tuck you in .

KLUTE: Get away from me. Don't you touch me.

POP: You better say your prayers son.

KLUTE: I knew I should have stayed behind. The whole time I said, Klute this man's cuckoo. I knew it when you sold the house, I knew it when you bought the pick up. I knew it was insane to leave Detroit. And I still don't know why you did it.

POP: I was hurt.

JULIE: *You* were hurt?

POP: Every time I'd roll down the car window by hand and not by pressing a button, I took it personally.

KLUTE: Big shot. He wanted a Mercedes. Blue collar grunt, he wanted what the rich folks have.

JULIE: We didn't need electric windows. We needed orange juice in the morning and mom cooking breakfast.

POP:(*Snapping at Julie:*) I guess I was oversensitive whenever the phone company called and asked for a payment. (*To audience:*)... when my kids sneakers didn't fit anymore and my eighteen percent interest credit cards were over the limit and my overdraft checking privilege was over the limit too and they were charging me a hundred dollars a month just for the interest and I needed gas for the car and the lighting company wanted to turn off the electricity. I was hurt. We couldn't even afford to see new movies and then we couldn't afford to rent old movies and we don't have the mortgage payment or the car loan payment and I didn't know how to get foodstamps and the rest of America don't know it yet but Detroit ain't there no more. Detroit's a rubble, bombed out like Berlin. People are leaving like hordes of the dispossessed.

Suddenly the big door slides open and Charlie and Vince come in from the blizzard with big chunks of ice which they throw into the giant pot on the massive stove. Steam bubbles up from the pot. Exhausted, Vince and Charlie begin to undress for bed.

VINCE: How the hell do these Eskimos fish through that ice?

CHARLIE: I don't know. How thick do you think it is?

VINCE: I'm just glad I'm not one of those fish under there, I'll tell you that. Charlie, you amaze me, how'd you find that lake in all that white out there?

CHARLIE: I guess I'm a good guesser.

VINCE: But people get lost in blizzards. They find them dead sometimes twenty feet from their houses.

CHARLIE: (*He goes to his father.*) Good night Pop (*Hugs.*)

POP: Good night Charlie.

CHARLIE: (*Goes to Vince, hugs.*) Good night Vince.

VINCE: Good night Charlie. (*Vince and Charlie go to bed, Charlie stopping to say his prayers first.*)

POP: Goodnight Charlie babe. Goodnight Charlie Chef-o-thenorth frontier. Goodnight sonny babe Charlie Chef-o-the-wild-frontier. (*Charlie and Pop spar a bit--Charlie goes to bed.*)

VINCE: Where are you goin' to sleep Pop?

POP: Don't know. Most of the time I sleep in the chair, tied up.

VINCE: Take my bunk.

POP: No I think I'll just sit here, while I'm feeling good and watch over my family. I know. When I turn out the lights, let's all pretend we're back in Detroit.

KLUTE: Will somebody please gag him?

POP: I used to go into the kitchen in Detroit when I couldn't sleep, make a cup of tea and go sit on the couch in the living room and just listen to the silence of my house with you kids asleep. Vince, you used to snore.

VINCE: I snored? (*Yawn.*)

POP: Yeah, a kid's snore you know, like... zzzzzzzzz zzzzzzz, soft and fuzzy like and I'd like it when the moon was bright, you know, shining on the rug, remember the big roses in that rug? (*They turn* *their backs to him and sleep.*) We still had those roses, Mom, and I in our bedroom when I sold the house, You older ones must remember when the whole house had those roses all over the floors. How big would you say those roses were? A yard wide? At least a yard wide, yellow, red, and blue roses in every room of the house. You know where we got that rug? Do you remember the R.K.O. Casino on Dartmouth Drive? When they closed it down there was a tag sale and your mom bought all the rugging. She intended to just cut a little piece out for our bedroom but they delivered the whole rug from the whole theatre over a thousand yards. The church people got some and the synagogue people got some and even the Nicholsons next door had those roses in their living room, still do, and I used to love those big flowers all over our stairs and in our bedrooms. We even had a piece in the kitchen. Loved it when the moon came through the windows at night because it made all the roses change to white, bright white, and dark white, all sorts of white and it reminded me of something...I can't explain... like a poem. My house was a poem and we're all asleep on top of giant white roses and I'd lay back and sip my tea and I'd feel the night holding us up, so safe and I'd listen to the breathing of my kids and my wife, all that breath goin' in and out, and I'd open the windows to let in some of that cool blue air and I'd imagine it going into your lungs, into your bloodstreams, the air of God, the air of the universe, sneakin' into our house on McCormack Street and takin' care of us. So glad I couldn't see the future them nights. Glad I was able to have hope, glad I couldn't imagine this cold place. I couldn't foresee anything to hurt us. Couldn't imagine anything that would dare (*Snorring, they have all fallen asleep.*) interrupt us. Vince...? (*Pop quietly puts on his snow shoes and outdoor clothes and whispers to Charlie:*) Charlie?

CHARLIE: Go away.

POP: Charlie wake up.

CHARLIE: Pop .

POP: Shhh. Get dressed son.

CHARLIE: What for?

POP: We're going hunting.

Joe Pintauro

CHARLIE: Wow .(*Charlie stirs and complies, putting on his shoes and overclothes. They quietly go to the sloding door. Pop turns off the light before opening the door. In the dark all of Vince's clothes hanging to dry, glow as if they are flourescent. The bread glows, hanging above the big pot and Vince himself, asleep and unawares, glows like an apparition.*)

CHARLIE: Ouuuuuu Chhhhhheeeeez! (*Pop opens the sliding door and we can hear the terrifying wails of the blizzard. It's night.*)

POP: You got the keys to my truck?

CHARLIE: Yeah. But Pop, look at what's happening. Vince is an angel.

POP: Don't wake them.

CHARLIE: Everything is shining, even himself. It's a miracle.

POP: Charlie, hurry. I've got to close this door. Quick, before they wake up.

CHARLIE: A miracle...a miracle at last.... (*We hear glorific music, then the lights go to black.*)

The music suddnely becomes the Red Hot Chili Peppers. As the lights come up warm and rosey, Mom is making breakfast. We hear Radio V.O.

RADIO V.O. (*Extremely rapid speech over music:*) Wake up cats it's Sam the dance man, early morning's favorite Disc-jock at W.Q.E.Z. Deetroit, annnd have we got news for you, every hour on the hour annnnnd have we got music, Yeahhh. Our own Madonna, Springsteen, Jackson annnnnd the Red Hot Chili Peppers. (*Copter sounds.*) What's that in the sky? Nothing but our own Red Hot shadow traffic Copter! Reports jam-ups on the Edsel Ford Expressway—Take the Davidson down to Lodge—I'm talkin' to you Mom fryin' those eggs, 'swell as you car phone freaks-when you hear this bell (*Bing.*) Dial 887, 6000, that's 887, 6000 'cause we got two wonderful prizes for the first callers: One: Dinner for 2 at Downtown Detroits famous Rattlesnake Club, part of the

beautiful Stroh Brewery complex right on the Detroit rivers...and
Two: weekend for two at the beautiful Troy Hilton, courtesy of the
Hilton Group, a chain of fine Hotels from London to Hawaii and
now the Red Hot Chili Peppers, brought to you by Dial-A-Mattres,
call 313-MA-T-T-R-E-S—leave off the last "S" for Savinqs—
Sealy, Posturpedic and many many more—The Red Hot Chili
Peppers....(*Music*.)

MOM: Come children, breakfast!

JULIE: Mom?

MOM: Wake up for God's sake. I've got eggs here and bacon
frying and I nearly sprained my wrist squeezing orange juice
for you all.... (*Klute approaches, not believing his eyes*.) Sit down
Klute. Those nails! Let me see. You're biting them again. Do I
have to put band-aids on them again? Julie, wake up your brothers.
(*She sings:*) 'Wake up family. It's your once a week bacon and egg
day in commemoration of the days of innocence and wonder
before cholesterol.' Now Julie one egg a week won't kill you and
in place of bacon, I've got you...guess what? Broooccoolleee!

CHRISSIE: (*Leaning against Mom, rubbing eyes as if it's an
ordinary morning*.) My feet are cold.

MOM: Hello, sleepyhead. Put your slippers on. Where's your
bathrobe? It's chilllleeee. Klute turn up the thermostat.

KLUTE: What thermostat?

MOM: You, don't give me that these eggs were kidnapped from
mother hens. They lay them once a day Julie and generously for
our benefit. You can't eat nothing but broccoli three times a day.
You'll produceenough gas to heat up all of Detroit for a year. I said
eat people. Go ahead, what are you in a trance or something? Eat.
You'll be late for the school bus. What time is it...turn up that
radio. (*Klute and the others look with suspicion upon the food,
refusing to touch it*.) Drink your juice dear. What's the matter?
What are you all staring at?

JULIE: You're...

Joe Pintauro

MOM: I'm what?

KLUTE: You're not supposed to be here.

MOM:(*Laughs a little reservedly. Their faces scare her.*)
Where...am I supposed to be?

CHRISSIE: Dead.

MOM: What? That's not funny. (*Klute turns off radio.*)

JULIE: Mom...you died.

MOM: Huh?

JULIE: You were killed in a car crash...

CHRISSIE: Head on collision.

KLUTE: Totaled the station wagon.

MOM: This is some kind of joke...So what's the joke?

KLUTE: You were coming home from work on your way to pick
up Chrissie and you drifted into the other lane...

MOM: No. That big truck...he drifted. I had no time...(*She puts
her hands over her mouth.*) Oh dear.... Oh.

CHRISSIE: We don't live in Detroit anymore.

JULIE: Look at the floor. No roses. You've been dead for two
years. Pop got fired and bought a new pickup and we moved up
here to Northern...

MOM: Northern...what? Montreal.

JULIE: Oh God no. Worse than that.

KLUTE: We're in a place so far up it's got no name.

CHRISSIE: Look! (*She slides open the door and shows her the* *howling snow.*)

MOM: (*Shuts door.*) Oh no, I must be dreaming...lookout... Oh God please let this be a dream.

CHRISSIE: Mom take me up to heaven with you.

MOM: What are you talking about? What heaven?

JULIE: Then where have you been?

MOM: Where have I been, I don't know.

KLUTE: Under the ground is where she's been. In the cemetery.

MOM: You'll scare her Klute.

KLUTE: Then where'd you come from?

MOM: I don't know but I would never have left you on purpose. Where's your father?

JULIE: He left with Charlie a little while ago.

MOM: How is my Charlie?

CHRISSIE: He's our cook.

MOM: Charlie can't cook!

CHRISSIE: And Vince works in a gold mine.

MOM: What gold mine? Where is my Vincent? Vincent?

VINCE: (*Waking up.*) Mom?

MOM: Oh Vince, look at you.

VINCE: You...you...oh, Mom. There are so many things I wished I'd said to you before the accident. If I had known...I woulda said so many things. (*They embrace.*)

MOM: Sit here. Drink this juice. Drink it, slow. Yes. Now tell me, what would you have said?

VINCE: (*Stares unable to speak.*) I...can't seem to think of it right offhand...

MOM: You...love me? Is that it? (*Vince shakes his head.*) But you've said that many times. All of you have.

KLUTE: I...didn't.

MOM: Of course you did.

VINCE: It's all the things we would have said if you hadn't died.

MOM: I died. I never intended to leave you...

KLUTE: Why didn't you pay attention to the road for cryin' out loud Mom?

JULIE: Yes. You were so stupid.

MOM: Do you think I had that accident on purpose? Are you crazy?

KLUTE: You were drinking martinis.

MOM: I had two.

KLUTE: Well it was cruel and thoughtless to me.

JULIE: Why *you*!

KLUTE: She was important to me.

MOM: This is the most unusual form of prejudice I have ever experienced. I've made some social blunder it seems.

KLUTE: It hurts. I'll never get over it. Never. Look where we are. Nothing to eat most of the time. Who's gonna come to our graduations and...our weddings. Who's gonna make me breakfast in the morning?

MOM: But I just made your breakfast.

KLUTE: Come on Mom. This stuff's not real.

MOM: Why not? I prepared it.

KLUTE: In an hour or so we'll all wake up and you'll be dead and I'll be hungry.

VINCE: Mom, touch my hair, like you used to, when I was a kid...give me your hand. (*He puts her hand on his head.*)

CHRISSIE: Me too.

JULIE: Mom... *She touches them all as they kneel at her chair, but Klute will not come near.*)

MOM: Klute....(*Klute almost begins to believe, then moves away.*)

KLUTE: You idiots. All of you. She's not here. Which one of you dreamt her up? Why don't you get out? You're just somebody's dream. (*She touches him comfortingly.*) Mom, I miss you...I miss you. Why are you torturing us?

MOM: I've got to get out of here before your father gets back.

VINCE: No. Why?

MOM: No. No. He can't see me.

VINCE: Tell us why?

MOM: Because one of you has dreamt me up and I want to end it before it upsets my husband.

CHRISSIE: Just let us dream a little longer, please, please, whoever you are.

MOM: Open the door for me Chrissie.

JULIE: But it's too cold out there.

MOM: I won't feel it.

CHRISSIE: Why?

MOM: Tell her somebody. (*Mom takes Chrissie to bed.*) Chrissie, please trust me. I have something very important to do.

JULIE: Will you come back?

MOM: Julie, darling, don't ask me that, please. (*Picks up breakfast.*) Now, Klute, open that door. Open it.

VINCE: (*He slides open the door, Vince brings Mom coat.*) Put this on...

MOM: No. I don't need it. Be good and Klute, I love you...(*Whispers:*) you were my favorite. (*She gives Vince a kiss.*)

She walks into the lavender light of the howling blizzard and disappears in the snow. the rosy lights of Mom's presence dissipate and the room returns to the gray, dark and cold hues of night. All are in bed except Vince.

VINCE:(*Shuts door.*) Who dreamed this? Me? (*It's as though he's sleep walking and he's the one who dreamed of Mom*)

Vince turns out light and goes to bed. The bread is still shining and so are Vince's clothes.

The dream Mother is gone but again we hear the door open and quickly shut again. Someone has entered. We cannot see them. The children are asleep. We hear the sounds of two men carrying a large burden. Lights creep up on the monstrous carcass of a twenty-four point reindeer lying coldly and dead upon the table, as if it is a holy thing. Its silhouette makes a powerful and overwhelming image on stage. One by one the children wake up and come to the reindeer and stare at it. They speak in hushed tones.

VINCE: Where did it come from?

CHRISSIE: Wow.

JULIE: Oh God no...no...

CHARLIE: What's the matter, it's only a reindeer.

VINCE: No Pop. You didn't. Charlie. He didn't...

POP: Now Vince don't go wimpy on me. You lost our food supply.

VINCE: I worked for it, but this is...this is...

POP: This is hunting. Ever hear of natural violence? Animals live off one another.

JULIE: Reindeer are vegetarians.

POP: If there was a lioness out there, starving. Wouldn't she attack this reindeer and bring food home to her cubs?

VINCE: A lion yeah, but a pick-up truck?

POP: I have no claws. I have no gun. All I have is that truck.

VINCE: How did you do it?

CHARLIE: It was neat.

JULIE: Men. You make me sick.

CHARLIE: Well it was sort of neat. We were on the road going through the pines and you know how the snow piles up on both sides of the road making it like a tunnel almost, we came upon this buck reindeer, he was caught in the tunnel and couldn't make it over the snow banks so we started chasing him. Man could he run, but we gained on him, and suddenly, he stopped short and looked us in the eye and wham! We nailed him. Pow. He jerked around for a few minutes, passed out and here he is.

JULIE: (*Julie goes for her coat. Charlie turns on the lights.*) You murdered this gorgeous beast. Oh my God I can't stay here.

POP: C'mere.

Joe Pintauro

JULIE: No-no. Don't touch me.

POP: Would you like to go into that soup. Here, let's put her in. (*He lifts her.*)

VINCE: Pop, put her down. Put her down.

CHARLIE: Oh my God, he's ready for another pill.

VINCE: Where are your pills?

CHRISSIE: Give him two. Quick.

VINCE: Pop, Take one of these.

POP: Romeo, wherefore art thou? The evil that men do lives after them. The good is oft interred with their bones, so let it be with Guildenstern.

VINCE: Drink pop.

POP: Et tu?

VINCE: Swallow.

POP: With this drink, I thee wed.

KLUTE: (*To Charlie:*) You Klunkhead. You expect to just dump this whole animal into the pot?

CHARLIE: We have to dress it dork head.

CHRISSIE: Here's my hat and scarf.

CHARLIE: He means cut it up Stuppo. Like skin it and make it into steaks. We can sell the head. They hang these heads in lodges and dens and with the money we can get Julie some grain and vegetables. Beans Julie, you can eat your heart out.

CHRISSIE: I think its still breathing. What if it gets up and starts to run around?

JULIE: Get that thing out of here.

POP: Vince, help me. Charlie, come on.

CHARLIE: Where to now?

POP: Grab a few saws and pass me those knives.

VINCE: What for?

POP: To dress the poor thing. Before it wakes up.

VINCE: Pop, you're a little confused...okay?

JULIE: He was better off when he thought he was Nixon.

POP: Just help me. Charlie cut there. Watch it now. Vince...you cut there. (*Vince gets into helping.*)

VINCE: You mean the head?

POP: Yes, we'll freeze the head and we'll advertise for a buyer. We'll skin the rest of it and make steaks. Get that tinfoil. We'll keep a whole leg o' deer for Charlie's soup. And the other leg for Christmas dinner.

CHRISSIE: But, pop... (*Vince gestures to Chrissie to be quiet.*)

The deer comes apart and they carry its pieces off.

JULIE: You primitives. You cave men. You never evolved any further. You're knocking yourselves out to be the biggest cliche in the anthropological chain.

POP: Where does MacDonald and Burger King get their hamburgers? Roy Rogers their chickens?

JULIE: From executing animals by the hundreds of thousands every day.

POP: That's because you don't listen when a carrot screams when you bite into it.

VINCE: Enough pop.

POP: You see those ends of asparagus and broccoli? Cut, decapitated, amputated from the stalk.

JULIE: Shut him up!

CHARLIE: Too bad we don't have a refrigerator.

KLUTE: The whole world's a refrigerator out there Charlie. It's a damn deep freezer. A million miles square.

CHARLIE: What if we bury the head in the snow?

KLUTE: Charlie, you're brilliance is blinding me.

CHARLIE: I take after my old man.

POP: Shut up! Klute, open the door. (*He does, Julie grabs her coat and starts getting dressed.*) Okay now Vince, more to the left. That's right. Out of the way, Klute. Good, we're doin' fine. (*They carry the carcass out into the blizzard. Charlie takes a leg to the store room.*)

JULIE: I'm coming with you.

POP: You take that coat off and get behind me.

VINCE: You're not dressed warm enough.

POP: Klute. You grab her and don't let her leave. (*Vince and Pop exit through the door into the blizzard with the carcass.*) Now close the door Klute. (*Klute only partly closes the door and obstructs the opening. There is only he, Chrissie and Julie on stage now.*)

CHRISSIE: Julie, why do you want to go out there?

JULIE: I'm going to try to find mom.

KLUTE: You're crazy. You'll freeze to death.

JULIE: No I won't.

KLUTE: I'll have to go out and find you and I'll get lost stupid.

JULIE: Oh, poor Klute. Well, I don't care. I won't stay in the house of thieves and road pizza ghouls.

KLUTE: He's your father.

JULIE: I prefer the blizzard to my family. Out of my way, Klute.

KLUTE: Bulldickey, Julie.

JULIE: I'll only die of hunger here.

CHRISSIE: Give her some of your dried papaya. Give her something to eat.

JULIE: Yeah. Put up or shut up. (*Klute steps aside.*) Cheapskate! (*She leaves.*)

CHRISSIE: No...Klute. Are you crazy? Julie...(*Chrissie goes out into the blizzard to follow her.*) Vince? Charlie? Jullllliiiieeee! (*Klute pulls Chrissie back inside and closes the door.*)

CHRISSIE: You monster, you reached the lowest rung on the ladder of civilization. You let her go rather than give up a stinkin' piece of papaya.

KLUTE: She's better off.

CHRISSIE: She's going to get lost and die.

KLUTE: We're all going to die Chrissie. What's the big deal? (*Charlie reenters, puts chunk of meat in soup pot. Klute warns Chrissie with his eyes not to mention Julie is gone.*)

CHARLIE: You know what I'd give my right arm for right now?

KLUTE: Go ahead. Make us throw up.

CHARLIE: Some onions and barley for that soup. (*Pop and Vince enter*) Pop, I got a great idea...

POP: Not now, Charlie, just bury that head in the snow. (*Charlie takes head outside.*)

VINCE: (*Holding his stomach, heads toward his bunk, sick and disgusted.*) And mark the place so we don't forget where it is.

POP: I feel so much better.

VINCE: I feel sick.

POP: It was hard for me too Vince. My children will eat and that's my duty.

VINCE: You're lucky you didn't run out of gas. What are you going to do now?

POP: I'll take a nap before dinner.

VINCE: I mean do about your hunting weapon the pick-up truck.

POP: Well we're just going to have to go out and get the gas and bring it here I guess.

VINCE: How far is the nearest filling station?

POP: Forty-five miles.

VINCE: Forty-five miles. You mean we're gonna walk forty-five miles in a blizzard, carry thirty gallons of gas for fortyfive miles back?

POP: I never thought of that.

KLUTE: That part's nothin'.

POP: What's the hard part?

KLUTE: Payin' for the gas.

POP: We got a fire going. For now soups cookin'. In a little while we'll have hot, hardy, meaty and delicious potage de reindeer. I brought home the bacon, now let's get some shuteye. Take your bed places everyone. When we wake up...we'll have venison soup with boiled meat on the side. Bye Bye baby bunting...(*Pop dances with Chrissie.*) Daddy's gone a hunting...

CHRISSIE: to catch a little rabbit skin... (*He lifts her up.*)

BOTH: to wrap his baby bunting in...

CHRISSIE: Mom was here.

POP: What? No Chrissie you dreamed it. You dreamed it sweetheart.

CHRISSIE: We all saw her. She went out that door with no coat on.

POP: Shhhhh...go to sleep. Shhhh...bye baby bunting. (*Chrissie tries to sleep. Charlie slips back inside. Lights go down.*)

We hear Natalie Cole's "Mona Lisa."

Slowly, silently, the door opens. The blizzard has calmed to a gentle peaceful snowfall so no one wakens to notice that a large, blue star, is coming into the space. Two figures accompany the star. It floats toward the table then settles. Iona has been carrying it. In her other hand is a set of reindeer reins.

JULIE: Sit here, Iona.

IONA: Thank you.

JULIE: As soon as I find the light you can turn off the star.

IONA: It belongs outside. Bring it back out there, Julie, and leave it where it can be seen from the sky.

JULIE: (*Julie has turned on a light.*) Sure.... (*She exits with the star.*)

VINCE: Who's there? Who are you?

IONA: My name's Iona. Your sister Julie brought me here to get warm. I'll be leaving in a few minutes.

CHRISSIE: Is Julie back?

VINCE: What? You mean Julie's been gone? (*Vince checks her bed, throws off the comforter and finds nothing there. Julie walks in and closes the door.*)

VINCE: Hey! Where were you?

JULIE: Out walking...

VINCE: In a blizzard?

JULIE: Well it has calmed down quite a bit. Hasn't it, Iona? There on the snow crust I see this blue star shining...like something fallen from heaven and when I got there, she was with it.

IONA: It's only a battery operated flare. Do you mind if I use my phone?

POP: What's going on?

CHRISSIE: Julie brought home an Eskimo woman.

IONA: I'm from Kentucky originally.

POP: Julie, are you alright?

JULIE: I'm fine. I found her with the star just walking in circles.

KLUTE: Out in a blizzard?

JULIE: Tell them what you were looking for Iona.

IONA: Norman. She's my animal companion.

JULIE: She?

IONA: Yes. Suddenly I felt no pull on the end of these reins and I realized that I'd lost her.

VINCE: Norman?

CHARLIE: Hi. (*Charlie goes to the pot with a big bowl and spoon and ladles soup into the bowl and stands there.*)

JULIE: This is Charlie, Klute, Chrissie, Vince and my father.

IONA: Thanks for helping me...

POP: Norman... She wasn't a....

VINCE: Yeah, she wasn't a...a...

JULIE: Yes...a reindeer. (*She knows it's Norman and wants to make them pay.*)

IONA: Norman wasn't just any reindeer.

POP: Excuse me I just remembered I have to check on...on uh...what was it Vince?

VINCE: Stay right here Pop.

CHRISSIE: Do female reindeer have antlers? (*Klute is laughing.*)

IONA: Oh *Yes!*

CHARLIE: Drink this while it's hot.

VINCE: No have some shark fin....Klute...? Please? (*Klute shakes his head no.*)

IONA: The soup will do fine. It smells wonderful. Thank you. (*Iona lifts a spoonful of soup, blows on it and waits. A helicopter sound starts coming closer and closer as she speaks.*) It must sound silly to you...(*Blows on soup.*), naming an animal companion the same as you would a human, but when Norman was born...(*Blows on soup.*)....the name Norman justed popped in my head, so who am I to argue with the unconscious? She'll be alright out there because reindeer know how to take care of themselves in snow storms a million times better than we do. Oh. (*The helicopter is hovering right over them*) Excuse me. (*She takes *out a portable phone and dials.*) Melissa? Iona down here.

V.O. MELISSA: I see your flare but no Norman for miles and miles.

IONA: Really? Well the snow's calmed down, hasn't it?

V.O. MELISSA: Iona, I have good visibility and I covered the area twice but there's no sign of Norman. I'll do another go around. Over and out.

IONA: That's funny.

KLUTE: It's only a another skinny caribou. There's hundreds out there.

IONA: You know, reindeer have big hearts. You don't know reindeer. A reindeer will sit in eighty below zero waiting for you outside your cabin till she freezes to death. They imprint on you and they're so faithful. If you fall down in a snow storm, she'll hunker down next to you and make a drift that holds the heat around your body. Better than a husband a reindeer. Loves you like crazy. She saved my life twice.

CHRISSIE: How?

IONA: Well, I was ice fishing. The ice cracked and I went under the ice, like this (*Kissing the sky.*) ....breathing...one inch of air. Can't make waves. Stay still, floating. Through the ice, I see her four legs over my face...tides pulling me, she's following over my face. The ice gets thinner, it's cracking. Splash! She's in the water. I grab her reins and she swims. On shore, I pass out from the cold. Next thing, she wakes me up in front of my bubble. How'd I get here?

CHRISSIE: She dragged you home. To...to your...

VINCE: Your bubble?

IONA: Yes. How would you feel if you lost somebody like that?

KLUTE: She thinks she knows everything.

IONA: But it's true. Human babies take so long to develop that we're grown men and women before we know how to take care of ourselves so we're still babies even when we're grown up. Gimme milk. Gimme money. Get-Get-Get. But when you learn to care about somebody else, you know, you protect them, help them, worry about them, you lose the habit of gimme, you know? It's like you finally pass on the light and you get used to the giving-giving-giving till you're not afraid to give up your body too. You simply die, and it's a pleasure really when you get down to it. Reindeer understand about dying. (*She's about to sip her soup.*) They sure know a lot better than we do. And if you're starving, why a reindeer would even give up his own body to feed you. They do it all the time.

JULIE: Don't drink that soup.

CHRISSIE: It's Norman.

IONA: It's Norman? I don't get it.

POP: I have no gun and I have no job. I have just one drop of gas left in my pickup. My children are hungry. I ran over him in the snow.

IONA: You ran over who?

POP: I ran over Norman. Your reindeer.

IONA: There was an accident?

POP: No. I deliberately ran over him.

IONA: What?

POP: I thought he was wild, honestly. I'm sorry.

IONA: (*Looks down at soup.*) Norman?

CHARLIE: Pour it back. Don't throw it out please. (*The children all surround Pop as if to protect him.*)

POP: We were a good family. They all had good clothes, they ate well, down in Detroit I had a pretty house with big roses...I don't know how to explain how we got here. I couldn't sit around and wait for the world to change when I lost my job. I was ashamed for the neighbors to see us fold up and fall apart. My wife was a proud woman...

VINCE: This is stupid Pop. You messed us all up. I can't believe our luck, having you as a father.

CHRISSIE: Leave him alone. You know he can't think straight.

KLUTE: No. He's having a lucid moment here. Let's make hay while the light bulb is shining in there. He dragged us up here to snow heaven, you remember Pop? It was Springtime in Detroit. You loaded the truck with us and you kept goin' till the houses got cheap and we bought this here, stupid snow cellar. He thought it was a potato barn. They don't grow potatoes up here. They just grow ice.

IONA: I feel sick...someone...Help me.

VINCE: Hold her Pop. Do something. Iona, there's not enough gas in the truck to take us to the nearest pump. We're up shit's creek without a paddle. You got to get us the hell outta here. When we finish eating Norman, it's gonna be curtains for us, believe me. (*No one can move.*)

POP: (*To audience:*) I always wanted that truck. As we were driving up here my heart was beating so fast...the further north we got the more I loved it. Those puffy white trees whizzin' by, swallows all zig-zaggin' in front of us and then open miles of meadow, all bright with wild poppies. I remember now, I felt free. All this land and no real-estate company in sight. God's earth, God's land, all free and plentiful. I felt proud to bring them here, proud to be alive in God's world with my kids, like a gift was given to me, like the world was given back to the people and we...we were the people. We were explorers, conquerors. I thought there'd be food. There's always food. Food is food. Food is supposed to be everywhere, isn't it?

IONA: You mean the kids are all hungry?

CHRISSIE: We're not hungry. We're starving. (*Ceremoniously, Iona goes to the huge pot. All are amazed. Charlie helps as Iona takes one bowl at a time and ladles out a bowlful for each of them. When all bowls are ready she passes out one for each of them. Charlie follows with spoons for everyone.*)

IONA: Vince. Charlie. Chrissie. Sit and eat. It's okay. Norman understands. Go ahead and eat now. Julie?

JULIE: I'm a vegetarian.

IONA: Well just for this once. Norman would be insulted. Please, it's very important. (*It's a difficult decision, but finally Julie takes a bowl.*) Good girl. Klute, for you.

KLUTE: Get that garbage away from me.

POP: Klute has his own food.

CHRISSIE: Stolen food.

IONA: No. Does he? Why he'd have shared it, wouldn't you Klute?

KLUTE: I would not.

IONA: I refuse to believe he steals without a purpose. Why do you steal Klute? Tell them.

CHRISSIE: He steals because he's evil.

IONA: I doubt that very much.

KLUTE: They say I steal because I miss my mother. Maybe that's true 'cause there's a big loss here. Big hole here and it's never gonna be filled, I know that. It's like losing an arm. Sure you're alive. You can talk, walk, eat but what do you do with the extra sleeve on your wedding day? Stick it in your pocket or fold it up here with a big safety pin and walk down the aisle? An empty sleeve, not like the others. You're a kid with a dead mother in the ground. She's not cooking or watching t.v. or telling you to clean up your room. She's stiff and dead and turning to compost in a box in the ground that can't keep out the water when it rains in April....

POP: Shutup.

KLUTE: No. What kid is supposed to handle that and a father who's depending on his medication just to know who he is?

POP: Your mother died a natural death.

KLUTE: It wasn't natural for me. For me it was an accident, a catastrophe, a fluke that ruined my life.

VINCE: Okay. How'd it ruin your life, Klute?

KLUTE: Vince, Geez, I'll never have enough. I feel owed to. I'm owed to more than all the goods and money in the world can pay me back.

VINCE: And I'm not owed to? Pop's not? All of us?

KLUTE: I got only one head, my own. I can only think for myself and feel for myself.

IONA: (*In an inspired, hopeful, trancelike state.*) Klute— I've seen space ships come over the horizon here at night. Nights so clear and empty that when the moon rises, a rabbit casts a shadow a mile long. You see shadows crisscrossin' on the snow crust, all those shadows crisscrossin' until the moon goes high and silver and then the world's so bright down here you can read a book by the moon. I wear sunglasses at night because the moon follows you on the snowcrust, the reflection. Shines bigger under your snowshoes than in the sky. You look up it's the moon, down, the snow's on fire.

VINCE: What kinda space ships?

IONA: Well...They helped us start a women's colony here....It's our underground, white halls, full of light. We have a president and vice president...and it's only women.

KLUTE: Is there one of Pop's pills left over for her?

IONA: Really. They've been tracking our planet for years waiting for our wars to stop.

POP: Who's been tracking our planet?

IONA: The folks from the stars who built our colony. They're going to help us reconstruct the world for the future.

KLUTE: Why do they base themselves here?

IONA: Cause it's empty and peaceful. The cold purifies the air. Only a few living things can survive, the strongest, the brave fish that swim under the ice, the sleek seals, the angry white bear and very few birds. Then there's us. They call us the angels of this area. It's all white and pure. You never see a mosquito or a cockroach. Mosquito would go bzzzzzzzzzzzzzzz. Ugh. Freeze in mid air in two seconds and drop. There's no water for insects to breed in up here, only ice. They like that.

JULIE: Vince fell into water that doesn't freeze.

IONA: (*Examines Vince.*) Oh you must have fallen into that creek behind that chemical plant where they make fluorescent paint.

CHARLIE: You mean it wasn't a miracle?

IONA: No. It's a bad thing. When animals drink there, they get white mouths and tongues that glow in the dark and we have to take them into our colony to detoxify them or they die.

VINCE: You mean, I could die...Iona take me with you, please.

IONA: Oh yes, we take men in an emergency like this.

CHARLIE: Only in emergencies? That's prejudiced against men.

IONA: Well our sponsors figure men haven't fixed the world yet so let the women take a crack at it. It's only a temporary thing. Don't get excited.

CHRISSIE: Right on sister.

JULIE: Right on sister.

POP: Shut up.

IONA: When anyone is in trouble, we're allowed to give sanctuary to any gender or persuasion but other than that, we're only women in the colony for now, sorry.

CHARLIE: Sounds like a boring place.

JULIE: Not to me.

KLUTE: Sounds double boring to me. (*Lie.*)

IONA: It's a lovely community. It's heaven.

VINCE: Where do you get your food?

IONA: We send the helicopter once a week down to Nitchequon and they come back with supplies. We have four chefs in the bubble, physicists, physicians, designers, farmers, tailors, musicians. We even have a hydroponic lettuce and spinach farm under grow lights.

JULIE: Do you have television?

IONA: No but everyone plays an instrument. We listen to National Public Radio at six o'clock and after supper, we tell stories to one another. It's nice. No commercials.

VINCE: What did you mean they call you the angels?

IONA: You too. Here's our wings. (*Snowshoes.*) Except we wear them on our feet. I'll tell Melissa to land and we'll take you to our bubble.

KLUTE: (*Eating soup.*) What is it a bubble or a colony?

IONA: The bubble's just to cover the entrance. No the whole thing is underground. (*Dials.*) Melissa? I'm coming aboard with some people. How many? Just a minute. Who wants to come? We can take three.

JULIE: Me. Please.

VINCE: I'll go.

CHARLIE: You go, Pop.

POP: No you, I'll stick around here.

CHRISSIE: He needs medication.

IONA: Do you have a prescription?

VINCE: Here Pop.

IONA: I'll have it filled if you like. We'll leave the blue star out on the tundra so we can find our way back. So that's one, two, we can take one more, two, if Chrissie would sit on someone's lap.

CHRISSIE: I'll stay with my Dad.

CHARLIE: I'll stay with my father.

KLUTE: Vince, can I go?

VINCE: What about your store room? (*No answer.*) ....Sure, come along.

IONA: Hello? Melissa?

MELISSA V.O. : Roger.

IONA: Melissa, radio the base to send some gasoline for a pick-up truck here to where the blue star is. Two ten gallon canisters should do it. And there are a lot of hungry people here so have them send a lot of vegetables. Over and out. (*Helicopter sound is heard.*) Well...are you ready?

VINCE: Ready.

KLUTE: I'm ready.

JULIE: Hang tight you guys.

Joe Pintauro

VINCE: We'll be back.

CHRISSIE: Will you?

KLUTE: Not me if I could help it.

IONA: Well goodbye, sir. Goodbye Norman.

CHRISSIE: (*Stops Iona.*) Goodbye Mom.

IONA: Well...Thank you. We'll be back. (*We see them leave in the snow and a helicopter light comes down and then they pile in. From off stage we hear them all shouting in unison as the copter rises.*)

Music from the movie: "Glory".

ALL: Whoooooaaaaaooooohh!/Goodnight..

POP: Merry Christmas to all and to all a brand new world!

CHRISSIE: Come back soon.

CHARLIE: Yeah...

CHRISSIE: Don't forget about us.

CHARLIE: We need you.

POP: (*Sadly.*) We need you so bad.

As the mysterious and triumphant music from "Glory" swells, the bright copter beam gets weaker and the sound of the copter going toward the new civilization, diminishes.

Pop stands stunned watching, then his face turns sour and sad, he stares into himself. The kids rush to Klute's bed where they start ransacking his goodies, putting on earmuffs, funny woolen hats and sneakers, all the paraphernalia that he had stashed away for himself. Pop stares at his kids in a sort of terror. He walks around the room taking in all that is there. He comes to the table and looks toward the door where the others had departed.

POP: Charlie. Will you come over here please?

CHARLIE: What?

POP: Did this really happen?

CHARLIE: I think so.

CHRISSIE: Oh no. Not again.

POP: Never mind. Don't mind me. Go on, eat. Have fun.(*He opens door looking into the far away tundra. In an inspired moment, he gets his coat, hat, gloves, scarf, and takes a chair from the table and places it in the doorway. He sits. Charlie and Chrissie look worried.*)

CHARLIE: What are you doing Pop?

POP: I'm going to keep my eye on that blue light. I'm going to keep my eye on that blue light...until they come back. (*The kids go to Pop and look out toward the light on the tundra, worried too now, that this latest episode in their lives has been an imagined thing. They hold each other as they look out to the blue star shining outside their house. Lights fade slowly, but the blue star only gets brighter, throwing it's light upon them as they stand in the open doorway.*)

END OF PLAY

Joe Pintauro

SIGHTINGS

by Brad Slaight

ABOUT THE PLAYWRIGHT

Brad Slaight is a writer, actor, and comedian. Originally from Michigan, where he taught high school for two years, he now lives in Los Angeles, California. Brad has written for television, including *ABC's Just The Ten of Us, Into the Night, Sunday Comics,* and *The Tonight Show.* His plays have been produced in Los Angeles and he has developed a number of feature film scripts. His many acting credits include: *Freshman Dorm, NBC's Funny People,* and the recurring role of Izzy Adams on *The Young and the Restless.*

Sightings and *High Tide* were written for and first presented by the Young Conservatory at the American Conservatory Theater (Carey Perloff, Artistic Director; John Sullivan, Managing Director), San Francisco, California, in July, 1992. The two plays were directed by Christianne Hauber.

The cast was as follows:
Sightings
JARRED .... Terrell Tangonan
JULIE......................... Stephanie Fujii
CHAD .... Eric Wolfson

High Tide
BRIAN......................... Paul Shikany
KEITH......................... Shayne Tolchin
LISA .... Melissa Adams
CONNIE .... Sherrill Snyder
TONY .... Joshua Costello

ABOUT THE PLAYS

When my brother first told me of his plans to encourage writers to address the young, I thought it was a challenge that I should be a part of. A section of my stand-up routine is devoted to Prom Night - something just about everyone can relate to - and so I chose that as the focal point of my play *Sightings*.

Originally, I had intended *Sightings* to be a very funny one-act, filled with crackling dialogue and hilarious punch lines. But Jarred and Julie, the two main characters, became far too interesting for that. Their innocence and emotions prodded me to examine them more closely. To look beyond the surface. As they progressed, I discovered important voices that needed to be heard, not just by teens, but by all ages. Jarred and Julie have been friends for many years, but the pressure of social acceptance has created a canyon in their relationship. It is an important night for both of them as they confront the truth about themselves and each other.

Being a runner in California, means that I have the opportunity to run outside a great deal. And since I live close to the ocean, my surface of choice is the hard packed beach created whenever there is a low tide. It was during one of my runs that I noticed a young man dressed in a suit and holding a surfboard. He was looking out at the water and didn't notice me as I ran in front of him. That image stuck with me for some time. I started to wonder why he was dressed like that. Did he plan on surfing in his Armani? Like most writers, I decided to fill in the blanks and create a story, predicated by that confusing image. *High Tide* is about two young surfers who have just come from the funeral of a close friend. They try to deal with the terrible concept of death, which seems even more painful when it involves a young person.

If there is a connection between *Sightings* and *High Tide*, it would have to be that they both involve young people who, despite the influences of the adult world, are on their own when it comes to dealing with the complexities of their emotions. Like teens in the real world, these characters must face their problems head on, no matter what the cost. So often society tends to treat the obstacles young people must face as insignificant. But if we all truly look back at those difficult years, we will remember just how important they were to defining what we have become.

Brad Slaight
September, 1992
Santa Monica

CHARACTERS

JARRED MORTON:	17. Likeable and odd. Concerned about where our planet is headed. Would give anything to make Julie happy.
JULIE MANNERS:	17. Pretty. Works at being popular. Moody. Cares for Jarred, but is afraid to show it.
CHAD MORRIS:	17. A self important stud. Nice building, no elevator. He can't believe Julie would keep him waiting.

Sightings

In the darkness we hear the sound of chirping California crickets. Lights come up slowly, but not bright since it is night time. We discover seventeen year old Jarred Morton, sitting in an aluminum fold-up lawn chair; next to him is a similar lawn chair. The chairs rest on a large circular piece of green carpeting. The setting is woodsy. Jarred looks up at the sky through a pair of binoculars. Checks his watch. He pulls a small radio from his nearby backpack and turns it on. Just in time to hear...

VOICE ON RADIO: "...even for the coastal areas. (*Pause.*) Still no relief in sight from those pesky Santa Ana winds, which, in addition to causing some rather dry conditions, seem to make people just a little bit crazy...or so the rumor goes. (*Pause.*) Lows tonight in the upper 60's and look for the heat to return tomorrow with temperatures nearing 100 degrees...for the fourth day in a row. And if that weren't enough, here's some real bad news - expect another first stage smog alert tomorrow."

JARRED: Figures.

VOICE ON RADIO: "Turning now to local news...three people were wounded last night in a drive by shooting. Police have several youths in custody and describe the incident as gang related..." (*Jarred shuts off the radio and returns it to his backpack. he looks up at the sky again, smiling at the beauty of it all, raises the binoculars to his eyes and aims them straight up with a jerky determined move.*)

JARRED: Even through the haze, I can still see the stars. No small miracle. (*He lowers the binoculars and pulls a small cassette tape recorder from his jacket.*)

JARRED: (*Speaking into recorder:*) TIME: 12:33 A.M. (*Pause.*) CURRENT CONDITIONS: Warm...with occasional violence. (*Pause.*) ESTIMATED TIME OF ARRIVAL: Soon. (*Pause.*) SPECIAL NOTE: Time is a variable. (*Pause.*) SPECIAL SPECIAL NOTE: Something worth waiting for. (*He finishes his comments and shoves the recorder back into his jacket.*)

175

GIRL'S VOICE (O.S.): (*Coming closer as she calls.*) Jarred? Jarred? Where are you? I know you're out here.

JARRED: (*Calling back:*) Over here!

GIRL'S VOICE (O.S.): Where is "over here?"

JARRED: In the clearing. On the other side of the pine trees. Just follow my voice. I'll keep talking until you find your way. Let's see, what should I talk about? How about drive by shootings? Or world hunger? There's so many exciting things happening here on planet Earth that I really don't know where to begin. Wait, I've got it...Homelessness. Now there's something I could really talk about... (*He stops on the entrance of Julie Manners. Julie is Jarred's age. She wears a prom dress, lots of makeup, and flashy jewelry.*)

JARRED: Great, you made it. Were my directions all right?

JULIE: You might have told me to bring a flashlight.

JARRED: I didn't think you needed one. It's a full moon. Nature's flashlight.

JULIE: Well it's not enough. I'm not a cat.

JARRED: Sorry. (*Drinking her vision.*) God you look beautiful. (*Adding.*) Even more than usual. (*She checks the bottom of her gown and notices a stain. Tries to brush it off.*)

JULIE: If I ruined my dress coming up here...

JARRED: I will assume full responsibility. Even though you can only wear that kind of dress once. After that it becomes just a memory in your closet.

JULIE: My Mother's going to shorten it next week so I can wear it to...(*A bit angry.*) Quit trying to distract me.

JARRED: I'm not trying to distract you. It is a very pretty dress. And you look very pretty in it. (*Quickly.*) And that corsage. Wow. Chad picked that out?

JULIE: They're orchids.

JARRED: Expensive.

JULIE: I wouldn't know.

JARRED: I do. I was going to send you orchids, but they were way out of my price range.

JULIE: (*A bit harsh.*) You shouldn't have sent me anything.

JARRED: The Florist did a good job with the carnations though. Did you like the arrangement?

JULIE: The arrangement...yes. The note...no. "Be here at midnight or you'll never see me again."

JARRED: I said be here at midnight, because it will be the last time you see me.

JULIE: Same thing.

JARRED: I don't mean to argue, but there is a big difference. (*Pause*)

JULIE: I should have called the police.

JARRED: Why? Is it a crime to send flowers?

JULIE: I was worried. I didn't know what you might do.

JARRED: Couldn't have been that worried. (*Looks at watch.*) You're thirty-six minutes late.

JULIE: How thoughtless of me.

JARRED: No harm done. I'm still here. (*Stands up.*) Here, sit down.

JULIE: I won't be staying that long. (*Julie takes her spiked heel shoes off. Rubs her foot.*)

JARRED: Those really are the wrong kind of shoes to wear up here. Although they look great with that dress.

JULIE: Will you stop.

JARRED: Sorry.

JULIE: You know, you've completely ruined my evening.

JARRED: I didn't mean to.

JULIE: I'm not so sure about that.

JARRED: Was it a good Prom?

JULIE: Besides feeling guilty about you all night, it was just fine.

JARRED: Guilty? About me? I don't think you understand.

JULIE: Come on, Jarred. I know why you're up here. And why you sent me that note.

JARRED: You do?

JULIE: You're upset because I didn't go to the Prom with *you.*

JARRED: I'm not upset that you turned me down. (*Thinking.*) Although I did ask you before Chad. However, a guy like me can well expect you to go with the more popular choice.

JULIE: Chad's popularity had nothing to do with me going to the Prom with him.

JARRED: I understand. (*Catches something out of the corner of his eye.*) Wait a minute? (*He grabs his binoculars and wields them skyward. He looks for a moment and then lowers them in disappointment.*)

JARRED: Sorry. False alarm. I thought it was them.

JULIE: Who?

JARRED: My ride.

JULIE: Your ride? I think you have your directions wrong...the road is over that way.

JARRED: They don't travel by car.

JULIE: Who doesn't travel by car?

JARRED: The Zuns.

JULIE: Never heard of them.

JARRED: That's what they call themselves. I guess we'd call them Martians, but that's just an earthling cliche. (*Julie looks at him for a moment. Jarred spots something in the sky and grabs for his binoculars again.*)

JARRED: Damn. That's what I hate about this spot. Too near an airport. But, that's just the way it has to be.

JULIE: What the hell are you talking about?

JARRED: Airplanes. All those flashing lights confuse me...

JULIE: No, back up. The part about the Martians.

JARRED: (*Correcting her.*) Zuns.

JULIE: Whatever.

JARRED: They're real touchy about their name.

JULIE: What the hell is going on here, Jarred?

JARRED: (*Explains.*) Tonight I will rendezvous with beings from another planet, and with any luck they will invite me to join them.

JULIE: Join them?

JARRED: Yeah, to go back with them to Zun. (*Excited.*) Boy, I can't wait to get off this planet.

JULIE: (*Angry.*) I'm really not in the mood for this.

JARRED: It's true. I swear. They should be here any minute. You'll see.

JULIE: No I won't, because I'm leaving. (*She starts out.*)

JARRED: You can't leave. You'll miss a chance of a lifetime.

JULIE: My loss.

JARRED: I'm not kidding around.

JULIE: Yeah, right.

JARRED: Julie you have to believe me.

JULIE: You want me to believe that a flying saucer is going to land here and pick you up?

JARRED: (*Laughs.*) Flying saucer? You've been watching too many movies. Actually, the Zuns travel in boxy shaped crafts. Kinda like Volvos, only bigger.

JULIE: All right, Jarred. You can cut this crazy act right now. Because I'm not buying it.

JARRED: What crazy act?

JULIE: You're not insane. You're just hurt.

JARRED: Hurt?

JULIE: Hurt because you didn't go to the Prom tonight.

JARRED: I would like to have gone. But it's nothing compared to where I'm going.

JULIE: (*Chiding.*) Well it's your own fault, because a lot of kids were there alone. So, I'm not going to feel guilty because you didn't have a date.

JARRED: I could never have gone alone. Too embarrassing. And rather boring. I mean all you can do is hover around the punch bowl and pretend like you're having a good time. And if you're a guy, you can't even dance. I've always wondered why it's okay for girls to dance together, but you never see a guy go up to a another guy and say, "Hey Bob, they're playin' our song...let's boogie."

JULIE: You're very strange.

JARRED: You're not the first person to tell me that.

JULIE: You're just doing this to get attention. And I don't appreciate it one bit.

JARRED: Julie, you sound so angry.

JULIE: Angry? Why should I be angry? I'm standing out in the middle of nowhere in my Prom dress.

JARRED: And don't think I don't appreciate that.

JULIE: I come all the way up here to see if you're all right...only to be insulted with some ridiculous story.

JARRED: The truth is often ridiculous.

JULIE: Jarred Morton, I don't ever want to see you again.

JARRED: If everything goes according to schedule, you never will see me again. (*Pause.*)

JULIE: This is some kind of sick joke.

JARRED: It's no joke.

JULIE: You've wasted enough of my time. (*Julie starts to walk away. Jarred gets out of his seat and heads towards her, but keeps an eye on the skyline as he chases her down.*)

JARRED: Julie don't be mad at me. Please.

JULIE: (*Stopping.*) I'm not mad at you, Jarred. Actually I feel sorry for you. Sorry that you have to make up a story like this just to get back at me for not going out with you.

JARRED: I'm not making this up.

JULIE: Good-bye Jarred. (*He blocks her way. She counters. He counters.*)

JARRED: Wait just a little longer. You'll see that I'm telling the truth.

JULIE: Get out of my way before I hurt you. (*Threatening.*) And you know that I can.

JARRED: Of course I do. I used to be your practice dummy. (*Jarred steps out of the way. Julie cools down a bit.*)

JULIE: Listen, Jarred, I really have to go. We'll talk about this later.

JARRED: No we won't. Because there's not going to be a later...I'm leaving soon.

JULIE: I give up.

JARRED: I've been waiting for this night all of my life.

JULIE: I have too. So why do you want to ruin it for me?

JARRED: I had no intention of doing that. I wanted to make this the greatest night in your life. (*Jarred crosses back to his chair, visibly saddened. He manages a glance upward before lowering his head. Julie starts to walk away, but stops and turns back towards him. She takes several steps in his direction.*)

JULIE: Jarred, I know you asked me to the Prom first. And I'm sure you think that I put you off until I got a better offer...I mean, until someone else asked me. But that's not true.

JARRED: It isn't?

JULIE: My friend Sandy knew I had a crush on Chad and was working on him to ask me out tonight. Planting the seed. That was days before you asked me. It just took him a little longer to get around to approaching me.

JARRED: So in a way, he asked you out first.

JULIE: Exactly.

JARRED: I understand.

JULIE: Do you?

JARRED: If you say it happened that way.

JULIE: That may be hard for you to accept. But it's the truth.

JARRED: It's not hard for me to accept.

JULIE: We can still be friends.

JARRED: I wouldn't have it any other way.

JULIE: And in time this will all make perfect sense to you.

JARRED: It makes sense now.

JULIE: (*Trying to convince.*) I came up here because I care about you, Jarred. You're very special to me.

JARRED: I know I used to be.

JULIE: You still are. (*Pause.*)

JULIE: Tomorrow we'll have a nice long talk. I'll make pizza. You can come over for a swim.

JARRED: Sounds great. But I won't be here tomorrow.

JULIE: Of course you will.

JARRED: (*Knowing smile.*) Well if I am...I'll come over.

JULIE: Don't stay up here too long. It's getting late. (*She starts to* *walk away)*

JARRED: It wasn't easy for you to tell me about Chad. And the fact that Sandy had to help you get a date with him...

JULIE: (*Stopping.*) I thought you deserved to hear the truth.

JARRED: And I guess I should tell you the truth about why I asked you out to the Prom to begin with. (*Julie looks at her watch, decides that she will hear him out.*)

JULIE: If it will make you feel better.

JARRED: We've lived next door to each other all of our lives.

JULIE: Yes, we have.

JARRED: Played together. Went to each other's birthday parties...well, most of them anyway.

JULIE: I mailed you an invitation this year. I swear.

JARRED: I'm sure you did.

JULIE: You know the postal service.

JARRED: Don't worry about it. (*Pause.*) Where was I?

JULIE: You were going to tell me why you asked me to the Prom.

JARRED: Right...actually I was building up to it. (*Thinks.*) Birthday parties...oh...right. We shared the same toys. We were in the same classes at school.

JULIE: I get your point. We've known each other for a long time.

JARRED: Right.

JULIE: (*Understanding.*) You asked me to the Prom because you were too shy to ask anyone else and you felt comfortable with me.

JARRED: Well...uh...

JULIE: I think that's very sweet.

JARRED: Sweet, but still not the reason I asked you out.

JULIE: (*Impatient.*) Why did you ask me out?

JARRED: I'm afraid to tell you.

JULIE: Afraid?

JARRED: You'll get angry again.

JULIE: (*Calmer.*) I'm not going to be angry with you.
Trust me. It's okay,

JARRED: The reason I asked you out tonight is that I want you to
go to the planet Zun with me.

JULIE: What!

JARRED: You said that you wouldn't get angry.

JULIE: I lied.

JARRED: That's okay. I'm a very forgiving person.

JULIE: Well I'm not. Zun? Jesus, Jarred. What kind of a fool do
you take me for?

JARRED: I don't take you for a fool.

JULIE: Then why are you doing this to me?

JARRED: What's wrong with asking you to spend your life with
me?

JULIE: On another planet?

JARRED: That's the best part.

JULIE: Jarred!

JARRED: There you go again.

JULIE: How did you expect me to react to something like this?

JARRED: I figured you would be confused, but not angry.

JULIE: Confused? You're the one that's confused.

JARRED: Julie, in all the years that we've known each other, have I ever lied to you?

JULIE: Knowing you, you've probably never lied to anyone. And maybe that's your problem.

JARRED: Then, why don't you believe me?

JULIE: Why shouldn't I? I mean, so many other men have asked me to spend eternity with them on another planet. Why not you?

JARRED: It's not eternity. However, we will live much longer on Zun.

JULIE: And they picked tonight...Prom Night...to swing by here for you.

JARRED: I admit, it was an incredible coincidence that the Prom fell on the same night as the rendezvous. That's when I decided to ask you out. I figured we could go to the dinner and dance and still be out here in time to catch a ride...so to speak.

JULIE: With the Zuns.

JARRED: Right.

JULIE: Who are going to be landing here tonight in their intergalactic Volvo.

JARRED: Any minute now. (*To himself:*) Maybe they're having a hard time navigating because of the smog. It could throw off their direction. (*Julie studies Jarred for a moment. Jarred continues his rational, talking to himself more than to Julie.*)

Brad Slaight

JARRED: What am I saying? A little smog isn't going to stop them. They're too advanced for that. Probably have a ray that will neutralize smog. No, they'll be here any time now. (*Jarred crosses back over to the chair area and looks up at the sky.*)

JARRED: (*Calling out:*) Citizen Jarred Morton of the planet Earth. Positioned at your predetermined coordinates. Ready for contact. Ready for contact. (*To Julie:*) It's not like them to be late. (*Julie watches as he waves his arms back and forth, as if to signal someone.*)

JULIE: (*A bit nervous.*) You're really serious about this.

JARRED: Of course I'm serious. They're going to be here. This is the most important night of my life. It's my destiny.

JULIE: (*Apprehensive.*) Jarred, are you feeling all right?

JARRED: Never felt better.

JULIE: At the risk of sounding like my Mother...Are you on drugs?

JARRED: I took a Sudafed this morning for my sinuses.

JULIE: Nothing stronger?

JARRED: Of course not. Why would I take drugs when I'm about to experience the ultimate high...interplanetary travel. (*Excited.*) And you know something else? They don't do a lot of exercising on Zun. So even though I'm not in great condition...I'll be considered musclebound. Won't that be nice? (*Jarred hears a noise and quickly looks to the heavens with his binoculars.*)

JARRED: (*Pause.*) If only my Mother could be here to see this.

JULIE: You're Mother?

JARRED: She's the one they were gonna pick up...but they'll just have to settle for me.

JULIE: Jarred, I really better go.

JARRED: (*Continuing his story:*) She made contact with the Zuns fifteen years ago tonight. On this very spot. They took her for a ride, but she didn't want to go home with them. (*Pause.*) Well, she did want to go, but I was still just a baby and she felt obligated to stay here with me.

JULIE: That was very thoughtful of her.

JARRED: She was the best. They told her that they would stop back on their way home...

JULIE: Stop back?

JARRED: It was a vacation vessel. Lots of tourists. Just tootling around the universe. Kind of a sightseeing excursion.

JULIE: A fifteen year vacation?

JARRED: Their time frame is different than ours. Kinda like dog years...you understand?

JULIE: (*Playing along.*) Uh...sure.

JARRED: So, since Mom couldn't be here, I'm gonna take her place.

JULIE: (*Like a shrink.*) Why do you want to go with them, Jarred?

JARRED: Because there's nothing for me here. (*Quickly.*) Except you. (*Pause.*)

JULIE: Jarred, I...

JARRED: (*Finishing.*) And that's why I want you to come with me. You're the only one that ever really understood me.

JULIE: (*To herself:*) That's a scary thought. (*To Jarred:*) Jarred, I think you need help.

JARRED: Not really. All I have to do is be at the prearranged location. (*Points to chair.*) Which I am? (*He crosses to chair area.*)

JULIE: Not that kind of help...(*Off what he has said:*) They're going to pick you up right there?

JARRED: Not actually pick me up. It's a beam. They catch me in a beam of green light and then...well it's very technical, but effective.

JULIE: A beam of light?

JARRED: Green light. And they'll take you, too. It's really no problem.

JULIE: But I don't want to go, Jarred. And I don't think that you do either.

JARRED: Come on, Julie. It'll be fun. We'll be treated like royalty there. We'll be happy for the rest of our lives.

JULIE: I'm happy here.

JARRED: Julie, you don't have to pretend with me. We go too far back. You're one of the most unhappy people I know.

JULIE: (*Defensive.*) I am not.

JARRED: You're moody. And I don't mean this as an insult, but sometimes you're downright depressing to be around.

JULIE: (*Bristling.*) Well I don't remember asking for your opinion.

JARRED: You weren't always like that. When you were six, you were like a little ball of sunshine. You couldn't wait for the start of a new day. And then the clouds set in.

JULIE: What are you talking about?

JARRED: You've forgotten so much. But I haven't. I remember it all.

JULIE: Remember all of what?

JARRED: The tree-house.

JULIE: The tree-house? I really don't have time for riddles.

JARRED: The tree-house, Julie. The tree-house your father built when we were six years old. The tree-house where we spent most of our childhood. Sharing secrets, making plans.

JULIE: Plans?

JARRED: Before our bodies changed.

JULIE: What's that supposed to mean?

JARRED: Before I became a disadvantage to you.

JULIE: That's very cold.

JARRED: Yes it was. (*Julie crosses back towards him. She is starting to boil.*)

JULIE: I never mistreated you, Jarred. We just grew apart. It's as simple as that.

JARRED: Simple?

JULIE: Yes. We weren't family...just friends. And friends sometimes drift apart. Playing together in a tree-house doesn't mean that we have to spend our entire lives together.

JARRED: We made a vow.

JULIE: What vow?

JARRED: When we were eight. It was August 29th. The hottest day of the year. We just got through counting profits from our lemonade stand. 67 cents. You took 33 cents and gave me 34. We talked for hours about what we would do with all that money. (*Remembering.*) You said that you were going to save yours to buy me a football for my birthday. (*He stops for a moment and looks at Julie. He smiles.*)

JARRED: Then you kissed me on the cheek and told me I was your best friend ever.

JULIE: (*Trying to cover her feelings.*) Well, I don't see what that has to do with anything...

JARRED: You and I made a vow that day. We vowed that we would *always* be together. No matter what.

JULIE: Jarred we were eight years old.

JARRED: There's no age limit on a promise.

JULIE: So you're holding me to a commitment that I made nine years ago?

JARRED: Not you...me. I'm holding myself to that commitment. Leaving here without you. That would be breaking my word.

JULIE: Leaving here...as in "leaving here with the Zoons?"

JARRED: Zuns.

JULIE: This is not happening.

JARRED: My Mother told me they have wonderful trees there. Sturdy trees. We could build a big house in one of them. It's a wonderful place to live. Safe. Happy. They don't have wars, or famines, or even smog.

JULIE: Listen, I have to go. Chad is waiting for me in the car. Now, why don't you come with me down the hill and we'll give you a ride back...

JARRED: (*Hurt.*) Chad? You mean you didn't come up here alone? I thought your date would be over by now.

JULIE: Well it isn't. (*Jarred pulls out a notecard form his shirt pocket. Scans it quickly.*)

JARRED: According to my calculations, you should have already ended your date.

JULIE: Calculations?

JARRED: I made a schedule of your evening. (*To himself:*) This makes no sense...I even allowed for making out. (*To Julie:*) You did make out with him, didn't you?

JULIE: That's none of your business.

JARRED: You're right. You don't have to explain your actions to me. (*Fetching.*) But considering it's probably the last time I'll see you and all...

JULIE: (*Out of frustration.*) Chad's taking me to his Uncle's cabin at Lake Arrowhead.

JARRED: Why?

JULIE: We're going to welcome the new day with a champagne breakfast.

JARRED: How boring.

JULIE: It's no spaceship ride to Mars, but I'm looking forward to it.

JARRED: On Zun there's a sunrise three times a day. We could take our pick.

JULIE: I'm not going to force you. But I really think you should let us give you a ride home.

JARRED: My home is among the stars.

JULIE: All right. I tried. (*Softer.*) Jarred, whatever is going on in your head...I really hope you work it out. (*She starts to exit.*)

JARRED: (*Desperate.*) Don't go, Julie. I'm not crazy. This is really going to happen.

JULIE: I have to go. I told Chad I'd only be a minute.

VOICE (O.S.): And it's been more like fifteen. (*Chad Morris, a well built seventeen year old, who wears a gaudy tuxedo, steps into the clearing.*)

Brad Slaight

CHAD: Jesus, why don't they put some lights around here. A guy could get killed.

JARRED: Actually, it's much brighter than usual. That's due to a full lunar exposure.

CHAD: What?

JARRED: Full moon.

CHAD: Who cares?

JULIE: Chad, I was just leaving.

CHAD: I know. I've been listening.

JULIE: You have? For how long?

CHAD: Long enough.

JARRED: So you know. Well, I'm sorry to disappoint you, but the Zuns won't want you to come along.

CHAD: (*Sarcastic.*) Awe gee, and I was all packed and everything.

JARRED: So I suggest you leave so that Julie and I can get ready for departure.

CHAD: She doesn't want to go with you. So I guess you'll be departing alone.

JARRED: If you weren't here, she might.

JULIE: (*Firm.*) Jarred, I'm not going anywhere with you. (*To Chad:*) Come on, Chad. We'd better go.

CHAD: (*To Jarred:*) I always thought you were weird. But this even surprises me. Jarred Morton...that's Jarred Moron. Wait'll Monday at school. Everybody's gonna know about you....Mr. Space Case.(*Julie starts to lead chad away.*)

JULIE: (*Concerned.*) Maybe we should go get his Dad.

CHAD: What for?

JULIE: I think he's having a nervous breakdown.

CHAD: Nervous breakdown, my ass. He's just plain nuts. That's what I think.

JARRED: You're too stupid to think anything, Chad. (*Chad stops.*)

JULIE: Don't pay any attention to him, Chad.

CHAD: Listen you freak... (*Chad moves in on Jarred. Julie, steps in front of Chad, trying to lead him away.*)

JULIE: Don't start anything.

CHAD: I ain't startin' nothin'. He is.

JULIE: (*To Chad:*) There's something wrong with him. He's not well.

JARRED: (*Hurt.*) Julie.

CHAD: (*To Julie:*) Why you takin' his side?

JULIE: I'm not taking sides. Let's just go.

CHAD: What's the hurry?

JULIE: We still have a long drive ahead of us. Remember, champagne...sunrise?

CHAD: Yeah, but it's only *ONE* sunrise. I mean we're about to witness contact from the unknown.

JARRED: I've known about them for years.

CHAD: I bet you have.

JULIE: Chad.

JARRED: It's okay, Julie.

CHAD: Listen to the boy, Julie. They could be here any minute.

JULIE: Let's go...now.

CHAD: Julie, I'm shocked. Jarred went to a lot of trouble to get you up here tonight. And now you want to run off and leave him?

JARRED: Julie if you don't want to come with me...I'll understand. You can leave if you want.

CHAD: Do you hear that, Julie? Jarred said that you can leave. (*To Jarred:*) What about me? Can I leave, too?

JARRED: I never invited you to begin with. I could care less what you do.

CHAD: I am crushed. (*Closing in.*) No, I'm sincerely hurt here. And after all I've done for little Jarred.

JULIE: That's enough, Chad. (*Chad circles jarred, who keeps an eye on him as he moves.*)

CHAD: Yeah, it is too bad your Mother couldn't be here to see this. Old Crazy Shirley Morton. She would have been real proud of her son, Crazy Jarred. Kinda runs in your family, don't it?

JULIE: Chad, will you stop.

JARRED: You have no right to talk about my Mother, you didn't even know her.

CHAD: Sure I did. I was your paperboy. Remember? (*To Julie:*) Julie remembers. Her house was on my route, too. Even then she had the hots for me. And we were only ten years old.

JARRED: I remember. My Dad fired you because you weren't reliable. We got a paper maybe three times a week.

CHAD: He reported me and they took my route away.

JARRED: He never told me that.

CHAD: Best thing he coulda done...I never liked that job, anyway. (*Pause.*) I especially didn't like goin' to your house. Because old Crazy Shirley would be starin' at me through the window. Givin' me the evil eye.

JARRED: She was probably just making sure you didn't steal anything.

CHAD: (*To Julie:*) From what I hear she used to stare at everyone. His old man never let her out of the house. (*To Jarred:*) Crazy Shirley Morton. The whole town laughed at her.

JARRED: She wasn't crazy.

CHAD: My Dad told me that she was always tellin' people about her encounter with the Martians.

JARRED: Zuns.

CHAD: She even wrote a book. But nobody would publish it. Bunch a' trash.

JARRED: Her book was a revelation.

CHAD: She had no proof.

JARRED: That doesn't mean it didn't happen. People always criticize what they don't understand. She was ahead of her time, that's all.

CHAD: Everyone knows that she died in the nuthouse up near Merced.

JARRED: It was a hospital. She died of cancer.

CHAD: Sure she did.

JULIE: Chad, you're being very mean.

JARRED: My Mother faced people like him all the time. He doesn't bother me. His type never do.

CHAD: My type? And what would that be?

JARRED: Doubters.

CHAD: Doubters? Oh, you got me.

JARRED: People who can't see beyond the edge of their nose. Empty minds that have no imagination. Empty hearts that have no emotions.

JULIE: Jarred, don't make things worse. (*Chad moves in close and with one sudden quick motion, he rips the binoculars from Jarred's neck.*)

CHAD: You don't mind if I borrow these? I didn't think so.

JARRED: Give them back...Now.

CHAD: Are you threatening me? (*To Julie:*) I think Jarred wants to fight me. He must be crazy.

JULIE: Leave him alone, Chad.

CHAD: (*Angry.*) Shut up, Julie! You've been tellin' me what to do all night.

JULIE: I have not.

CHAD: We're up here with Crazy Jarred, aren't we? Sure wasn't my idea.

JARRED: She didn't know anything about this. I just told her. (*Chad looks up through the binoculars at the sky.*)

CHAD: Looks like any other night to me.

JARRED: How would you know what any night looks like?

CHAD: You think you're the only one that owns a pair of binocu...(*Excited.*) Wait, what's that? Oh my God...it looks like a spaceship?

JARRED: I'm not amused.

CHAD: (*Startled.*) No, I'm serious. I see somethin'. And it sure ain't an airplane!

JARRED: (*Cautious.*) Really?

CHAD: Really. But it's not saucer shaped or anything.

JARRED: Box shaped...is it box shaped?

CHAD: Exactly. It's coming this way. This is incredible. (*excited*) You were right! My God, you were right! (*Jarred can no longer contain himself and takes the binoculars from Chad. He looks straight up.*)

JARRED: I can't see anything.

CHAD: To the left...look to the left. (*Jarred turns to the left, Chad counters to the right, positioning himself behind Jarred.*)

JARRED: I still can't see anything.

CHAD: It's there ! I saw it. (*Jarred twists around, trying to get a fix on what Chad saw. In the process he falls over Chad, who quickly maneuvers on top of Jarred, pinning him to the ground.*)

JARRED: Get off!

CHAD: (*To Jarred:*) I'm not through with you yet. (*To Julie:*) Watch the skies for us, in case they try to land.

JULIE: You can cut the macho routine, Chad. I'm not impressed.

JARRED: It's okay, Julie. I'm not afraid of him.

CHAD: Well you better be, you little freak. Because after tonight you're gonna wish to God that a spaceship had picked you up.

JULIE: He's got enough problems. Leave him alone. (*Julie crosses* *to Chad and tries to pull him off. He throws her aside.*)

CHAD: Stay out of this! This is between him and me. Just stay out.

JARRED: (*Squirming to get free.*) Don't you dare treat her like that.

CHAD: (*to Jarred*) You must have a little bone on for her pretty bad to pull a stunt like this. And I can't really blame you...I heard she's great in bed...a real screamer.

JARRED: (*Very upset.*) You better watch your mouth.

CHAD: Finally hit a nerve, huh? Don't care what I say about your Mother, but Julie...well, she must mean quite a bit to you.

JARRED: (*Fighting.*) Let me up and I'll show you just how much she means to me.

CHAD: Don't tell me you haven't heard about Jumpin' Julie. (*Suggestive laugh.*) She'll "jump in" to bed with anybody.

JULIE: I'm leaving.

JARRED: (*To Chad:*) Why would you say such a terrible thing? It's me who you're mad at. Not her.

CHAD: Because it's the truth. And since everybody is bein' so truthful tonight. Well, I thought I'd throw somethin' into the pot.

JARRED: Julie's not that kind of a girl.

CHAD: Maybe not for dorks like you. But just about everybody else in school.

JARRED: You're lying. (*To Julie:*) Julie, tell him he's lying.

CHAD: (*To Jarred:*) Where have you been? Do you actually think I asked her out because I liked her? I can have anybody I want. I took her to the Prom because I didn't want to spend all that money and get nothing in return. She's a sure thing. (*Pause.*) As far as the other guys are concerned, tonight isn't a date...it's just my turn.

JULIE: You bastard.

CHAD: (*to Jarred:*) Gee, maybe after I'm through with her, I'll bring her back here so the two of you can have a little romp in the tree-house. (*Jarred stops struggling. Chad looks at him and laughs at the conquest.*)

JULIE: You can go to hell, Chad Morris.

CHAD: He's crazy anyway. What does it matter? (*Chad stands to his feet and crosses over to Julie. Jarred remains motionless, his will to fight is now gone.*)

CHAD: (*To Julie:*) Let's get out of here. We've already wasted too much time. (*He crosses to Julie and starts to lead her away.*)

JULIE: (*Pushing him off.*) I can't believe you said that.

CHAD: I can't believe he didn't know. (*They have their backs to Jarred and cannot see him as he stands to his feet. He runs towards Chad and gives him a push, knocking him to the ground.*)

CHAD: You've had it now you little nutcase. (*Chad crosses towards Jarred, who is ready to fight. Julie steps in the middle.*)

JULIE: Jarred, fighting is everything you're against. I think it's very sweet that you want to protect me, but he's not worth it.

JARRED: It's the only thing he understands.

JULIE: True, but this isn't your fight...it's mine. (*With that Julie turns and jerks her knee up into Chad's groin. A very professional and effective move. Chad rolls on the ground in agony.*)

JULIE: (*To Chad:*) You want more? Because that was a very basic move. I'd just love to show you some of the more advanced methods I've mastered. (*Chad rises to his feet. Slowly. Painfully.*)

CHAD: You're as crazy as he is.

JULIE: You better believe it. (*Julie lunges at Chad. He makes a quick exit - as quick as he's able - holding his crotch as he goes.*)

CHAD: *(As he goes.)* I'm not through with you, Morton. Come Monday...you're a dead man.

JULIE: And so are you if you so much as touch him. *(Chad exits. Julie crosses to Jarred, who is a bit stunned by what has just happened.)*

JULIE: Are you all right?

JARRED: I'm fine. I hope he'll be all right.

JULIE: He'll live.

JARRED: I can't believe I was actually ready to fight him. I've never felt like that in my life.

JULIE: Chad brings out the worst in people. *(Julie crosses to the chair. Contemplates sitting in it, but remembers the significance of its position and sits instead on edge of the green carpet.)*

JARRED: This is all my fault. If you hadn't come up here, you'd be on your way to Lake Arrowhead.

JULIE: There's only one reason that he wanted to take me there. And it wasn't because of the mountain air.

JARRED: I want you to know that I don't believe what he said about you.

JULIE: I appreciate that. *(Pause.)*

JARRED: Because, of course, it isn't true. *(Long Pause..)*

JULIE: I have this insecurity problem. But it always seems to work against me. Especially with boys.

JARRED: We're not all like Chad.

JULIE: I know. Just the ones I date. I've only gone out with a few guys, but when you're my age that's enough to earn you a reputation.

JARRED: We're all insecure.

JULIE: Sometimes I wish I would have stayed six years old...forever.

JARRED: That's how I will always see you. (*Jarred crosses and sits in the chair.*)

JULIE: What you and I have must be very special, Jarred. Because when Chad was telling you about me...I was ashamed. Not about what he was saying. But that he was saying it to *you*.

JARRED: We do have something special, don't we?

JULIE: Maybe you're not so crazy. Maybe coming up here tonight was the best thing that's happened to me in a long time.

JARRED: I was hoping for that. (*Sincere.*) Change your mind and go with me.

JULIE: (*Smiling.*) To Zun?

JARRED: Yes.

JULIE: Jarred, you have my attention now. And my respect. Do you still think you have to go there?

JARRED: It's my destiny. It's what I've waited for all my life.

JULIE: Maybe you should talk this over with your Dad. He could help you.

JARRED: He knows all about this. All those years he stood by my Mother. Well, let's just say that tonight will be payback time.

JULIE: So you're still sticking with this story?

JARRED: It's not a story. Come with me? It's so much better where I'm going. (*Julie crosses over to Jarred and looks at him for a moment. She kisses him on the cheek.*)

JULIE: You're my best friend ever. (*Pause.*) I hope you find what you want...wherever you're going.

JARRED: And I hope you find what you want. Right here.

JULIE: I think we both will.

JARRED: Good-bye, Julie.

JULIE: The invitation still stands for tomorrow. You know, pizza and a swim. I would really like to see you.

JARRED: I'll keep that in mind.
they both stare up at the sky for a moment.

JULIE: It's so warm.

JARRED: Santa Ana winds...I hear it makes people act a little crazy.

JULIE: Nothin' wrong with being a little crazy.

JARRED: My bike is hidden in the bushes over there. Go ahead and ride it home. I won't need it anymore.

JULIE: No thanks. I could use the walk.

JARRED: Julie, at night...when you look up at the stars. Think of me.

JULIE: I'll see you tomorrow. (*She starts to walk away; stops and turns to him.*)

JULIE: Jarred, I do remember. I remember the tree-house.

JARRED: Thank you. (*She turns her back on Jarred and with renewed determination starts to head off into the night. And then stops. Something has caught her attention. She looks straight up at the sky. Jarred turns and looks at her with a smile. They both freeze in those positions.*

The lights fade to pinspots on each of them for a few moments - Jarred looking at Julie, as Julie looks at the sky - and then the lights fade to black.)

THE END

Brad Slaight

HIGH TIDE

by Brad Slaight

CHARACTERS

BRIAN PRESSMAN: 18. But acts older. Feels that there is no one he can turn to in this moment of grief and confusion.

KEITH KOLE: 17. Surf dude. Looks up to Brian the same way he looked up to Kirk. Says whatever is on his mind.

CONNIE: 17. A tourist from Ohio. Plain looking. Brian confides in her and she listens.

LISA: 16. Another tourist from Ohio. Connie's friend. Looking for a tan and a man.

TONY: 22. A California Lifeguard. Feels bad about what happened to Kirk.

SETTING

A southern California beach. Late fall.

High Tide

In the darkness we hear the sound of the ocean, overtaken by the sound of a loud hard rock song. As the lights come up, we discover Brian Pressman, a young looking eighteen year old. He is barefoot and wears a suit and tie. Standing next to Brian, and holding a large music boom box, is seventeen year old Keith Kole; he also wears a suit. Keith tries to sing along with the song, but doesn't know all the words so he hits the ones he can, and hums the rest. The song finishes. Both of them continue to look out at the ocean.

KEITH: That was Kirk's favorite song.

BRIAN: I know.

KEITH: I wanted to play it today, but Reverend Parks said it wouldn't be right...'cause we were in church and all.

BRIAN: Sounds like something he'd say.

KEITH: Seems to me that a guy should be able to hear his favorite song at his own funeral.

BRIAN: He couldn't hear it anyway.

KEITH: You know what I mean. *(They stare out at the ocean for a moment. During their silence we will notice the surroundings: a previous high tide has pounded out a natural shelf of heavy packed sand, which rises approximately two feet from the shoreline. A gentle slope towards stage left will give the staging enough variety in the absence of furniture. A trash barrel stands nearby wearing a faded advertisement from a local radio station. Scattered about the sand is the usual refuse left behind by those who could care less.)*

KEITH: Sure crowded there today.

BRIAN: Yup.

KEITH: Two hundred and twelve people. My brother counted.

BRIAN: Really?

KEITH: It means a lot to the family. You know, seeing that he had so many friends and all.

BRIAN: I suppose.

KEITH: Lotta crying.

BRIAN: Uh huh.

KEITH: I even cried. (*Pause.*) And I never cry. But when Mrs. Woodman was brought in and she had to be helped to her seat. Wearin' shades to cover her eyes...dressed all in black. I mean it really hit me. Kirk's gone. And she knew it.

BRIAN: Yes, Kirk is gone.

KEITH: Good thing his Dad kept it together. If he woulda lost it, everybody woulda been on their asses.

BRIAN: You're probably right. (*Pause.*)

KEITH: Wish it wouldn't have been an open casket.

BRIAN: Me too.

KEITH: My Mom said it was good for everyone to see the body. So we see that he's really dead.

BRIAN: I could have done without it.

KEITH: I didn't want to look at him at first, but when I did...it was like I couldn't stop. It looked like he was sleepin', but his chest wasn't movin'. I couldn't stop lookin' at his chest. Just didn't move.

BRIAN: I wondered why you stood there so long.

KEITH: I thought it was stupid that they dressed him up. Kirk never wore anything but jeans and stuff. They shoulda put him in a wet suit. That woulda been more natural.

BRIAN: You're right. (*Pause.*)

KEITH: Reverend Parks' speech was way off, too.

BRIAN: You mean the eulogy?

KEITH: Parks didn't even know him. I think Kirk stopped goin' to church when he was seven.

BRIAN: Kirk used to say that the ocean was heaven, and the shoreline was his altar.

KEITH: That's the kinda stuff we shoulda heard today.

BRIAN: There were a lot of things we should have heard today. (*Pause.*)

KEITH: I almost said something when we were at the cemetery. You know, when everyone was just sittin' there staring at the coffin. I wanted to tell them what Kirk was really all about.

BRIAN: Why didn't you?

KEITH: Guess I kinda dogged out.

BRIAN: I don't think that anybody really knew what Kirk was all about.

KEITH: We did...we were his friends.

BRIAN: We hung out together. Played together. But I don't think we really knew Kirk.

KEITH: Well if anyone did...it was you. He was my best friend, too...but I think you knew more about his feelings.(*Brian is bothered by that.*)

BRIAN: Look, I knew his favorite foods, choices in women, that kind of stuff. But I didn't know what made him tick.

KEITH: I meant it as a compliment.

BRIAN: (*Irritated.*) I only knew what he wanted me to. He was an enigma.

KEITH: A what?

BRIAN: A man of mystery.

KEITH: Oh.

BRIAN: He played me, just like he played everyone else. Nobody could figure him out.

KEITH: Well he was still a good guy. Always did right by me.

BRIAN: I didn't say he wasn't a good guy. (*pause.*)

KEITH: Well it's over now. He's gone, bro'.

BRIAN: Yup. (*They look out at the water in silence for a few moments.*)

KEITH: You wanna swim out there?

BRIAN: No.

KEITH: Me neither. Who knows...same thing might happen to us if we did.

BRIAN: I don't think so.

KEITH: Maybe this next summer we will. When the surf isn't so rough. We could drop a memorial marker or somethin'. You know, where he went down. Or at least where we think he went down.

BRIAN: He was pretty far out.

KEITH: Too far out. That sure wasn't like him.

BRIAN: No, it wasn't. (*Pause.*)

KEITH: Why did he have to come out here alone?

BRIAN: He had his reasons.

KEITH: If one of us would have been with him, this never would have happened.

BRIAN: But it did happen. Kirk chose not to include us and there's nothing we can do to bring him back. *(Keith crosses to the incline and sets the stereo down. He rummages through a backpack and pulls out a pack of cigarettes.)*

BRIAN: I thought you quit.

KEITH: I did...but I really need one now. Want one?

BRIAN: No. *(Keith lights up and enjoys his smoke alone.)*

KEITH: I slipped five bucks in his jacket.

BRIAN: What?

KEITH: When no one was lookin' I slipped five bucks in Kirk's jacket.

BRIAN: Why?

KEITH: 'Cause I owed it to him.

BRIAN: I don't think he's really gonna need it.

KEITH: I owed him five bucks. Didn't want him to go out thinkin' that I was lame.

BRIAN: If it made you feel better.

KEITH: Just tyin' up loose ends, bro' *(Pause.)*

KEITH: This is my first funeral. Well, first one I remember. My Grandpa died when I was three, but that doesn't count.

BRIAN: It did for your Grandma.

KEITH: I'm tryin' to make a point here.

BRIAN: I'm not stopping you.

KEITH: It's like we lost more than Kirk. We lost a part of ourselves. I'll never be the same again. That's for sure. And I'll never forget the Kirker. (*He crosses over to Brian and puts his arm around him. Brian pulls away.*)

BRIAN: Don't!

KEITH: What'd I do?

BRIAN: For the past two days everybody has been touching me. Hugging and patting me on the back. Like it means anything.

KEITH: People just want to show that they care. And want to help you through the loss.

BRIAN: They have no idea what loss means.

KEITH: Maybe they don't, but I do. He was my friend too, Brian. And I'm hurtin' right now.

BRIAN: Blame Kirk. (*Keith stares at Brian for a moment.*)

KEITH: What's with you? It's like you're pissed about all of this. Like you're mad at Kirk.

BRIAN: Maybe I am.

KEITH: What for? I don't understand you sometimes, Brian.

BRIAN: I'm not asking you to understand me.

KEITH: We need to stick together. God, we're friends. Don't shut me out.

BRIAN: Kirk is the one that shut us out. He came down here alone and that's how he left us.

KEITH: Let's not argue...Kirk hated it when we argued. (*Keith crosses over to the trash barrel and puts out his cigarette. notices the debris and starts to pick it up. Brian crosses to ledge and* *sits down. He takes an envelope out of his jacket pocket and looks at it, looks over at Keith and then puts it back in his pocket.)*

KEITH: This place looks worse than my bedroom. Damn tourists!

BRIAN: What makes you think it's tourists?

KEITH: Because this is the kind of stuff that they do. Come to our beach and mess it up. What do they care?

BRIAN: Our beach?

KEITH: Kirk hated tourists, too. Remember what he called them?

BRIAN: Turdists.

KEITH: (*Laughs.*) Turdists...perfect description. Mr. Woodman used to get so mad when he'd say that...'specially when he said it at the restaurant. (*Imitates.*) "Kirk...those people you hate so much put clothes on your back and are the reason you'll be able to go to college." Like he wanted to go to college.

BRIAN: He did.

KEITH: Yeah, right.

BRIAN: Really. Kirk wanted to be a writer. Probably would have done real well in college.

KEITH: A writer? No way. I've seen his report card. Worse than mine.

BRIAN: Some of the most creative people that ever lived bombed out of high school.

KEITH: Kirk never told me he wanted to be a writer.

BRIAN: Lot of things he never told any of us.

KEITH: He did have a way with words...What did he write about?

BRIAN: The beach, mostly. Poems about the beach.

KEITH: Poems?

BRIAN: Free verse.

KEITH: He ever write anything about me?

BRIAN: I don't know.

KEITH: I'd like to read some of his stuff. Do you have them?

BRIAN: Why would I have them?

KEITH: You knew he wrote them. You're one up on me.

BRIAN: I don't know what he did with them. Threw them away for all I know.

KEITH: I'll ask his Mom. She's probably got them.

BRIAN: I doubt it. (*We hear a commotion coming their way. Keith and Brian look down the shoreline.*)

KEITH: Ladies, due South.

BRIAN: Noisy ladies.

KEITH: Comin' this way.

BRIAN: Let's go.

KEITH: Remember our motto: Never leave until you see the whites of their thighs.

BRIAN: Today's different. Look, I asked you down here because I wanted to talk to you about something. Away from people.

KEITH: I think we should go for it. In honor of Kirk. He would want us to. It's what he woulda done, bro'.

BRIAN: This is your idea of a fitting tribute?

KEITH: Somethin' like that.

BRIAN: They could be tourists.

KEITH: They could be good looking tourists. (*Keith steps down center and stares at the approaching girls. Brian stays seated on the incline.*)

KEITH: One of them is limping...you can have her.

BRIAN: Thanks. (*Keith looks again.*)

KEITH: I think they are tourists. Either that, or one of them actually has giant mouse ears.

KEITH: Their comin' over here. Be cool.

BRIAN: It's a struggle. (*Keith gives them one last look, and as they approach he looks off in the other direction, pretending to be unaware of their existence. Two teenage girls come into view. They move slowly since one of the girls is hobbling along on her one good foot. Lisa, a somewhat attractive teenette who wears more makeup than clothing and a set of mouse ears from Disneyland, helps her friend Connie, towards Brian and Keith.*)

LISA: Can you guys help us?

KEITH: You talkin' to us?

LISA: Do you see anyone else around here?

KEITH: Nice attitude.

LISA: My friend cut her foot. She may need stitches. (*Keith crosses to Connie and helps her to the incline. Brian doesn't want to get involved and is not pleased when she sits next to him.*)

CONNIE: We were looking for a lifeguard, but couldn't find one.

LISA: Yeah...what kind of a beach is this? No sun. No lifeguards.

KEITH: You guys must be from out of town.

LISA: What's that supposed to mean?

KEITH: It means what it means.

LISA: See, Connie, I told you guys in California were deep.

BRIAN: What happened to your foot?

CONNIE: I stepped on a piece of glass, but I'm going to write shark attack on my postcards.

LISA: Some beach you got here.

KEITH: Don't blame that on us locals.

BRIAN: We've had some storms...Brings a lotta junk down from the hills. (*Keith crosses to Connie and looks at her foot.*)

KEITH: Don't think you'll need stitches.

LISA: Gee, Connie...aren't we lucky that we ran into a doctor?

KEITH: You gotta be from New York.

LISA: Ohio.

KEITH: Same thing. Anything east of Nevada is attitude country.

BRIAN: You really should wear shoes around here. The sand is like a mine field.

CONNIE: Shoes and more clothes. Somehow I thought California was warm.

KEITH: It's almost winter here.

LISA: We must have passed twenty lifeguard towers...all of them empty.

BRIAN: It's off season.

LISA: You wouldn't happen to have any medical supplies...like maybe in your car?

KEITH: Yeah...we drove down here in an ambulance.

CONNIE: I think you met your match, Lisa.

KEITH: Lisa? Sounds like a California name to me.

LISA: Don't you wish.

CONNIE: God, I'm cold.

LISA: Cold? How can you be cold at the beach?

CONNIE: I can be cold anywhere when there's no sun. (*Keith takes his jacket off and hands it to her.*)

CONNIE: You need it.

KEITH: Nah, I'm plenty warm.

CONNIE: You sure?

KEITH: I'm a surfer. (*Cocky.*) Cold...I don't know the meaning of the word.

CONNIE: Thanks. (*She takes it and wraps it around her shoulders.*)

KEITH: (*To Lisa:*) You want Brian's jacket? (*Brian shoots him a look on that.*)

LISA: No way...I spent over sixty bucks for this swimsuit and I'll be damned if I'm gonna cover it up. (*Keith takes off his tie.*)

KEITH: (*To Connie:*) Here, you can use my tie...you know, as a tourniquet?

LISA: It's a cut. I don't think she's gonna bleed to death or anything.

CONNIE: Thanks anyway.

BRIAN: A tourniquet?

KEITH: So I flunked my Red Cross training.

CONNIE: This whole day has been a disaster.

LISA: Even Disneyland. Hardly anybody there.

BRIAN: That's the best time to go. No lines.

LISA: I like lines.

BRIAN: You like lines?

LISA: Yeah, good way to meet people.

KEITH: Yeah...I meet all my dates on the Pirates of the Caribbean. *(Connie laughs at that. Lisa shoots her a look. Keith rolls up his tie and sticks it in his jacket pocket.)*

LISA: You guys always wear suits when you come down to the beach?

KEITH: No...today's kinda different. *(There is an awkward pause. Keith looks at Brian, who stares at the ground in silence.)*

KEITH: We just came from a funeral.

LISA: Who died?

CONNIE: Lisa!

KEITH: One of our buds. He was only seventeen.

CONNIE: Sorry.

KEITH: Yeah.

LISA: What happened to him?

KEITH: Drowned. *(Points.)* Right out there somewhere. *(Connie, Lisa, and Keith look out at the ocean.)*

LISA: I never knew anyone who drowned before.

CONNIE: Lisa, will you stop?

LISA: I'm not being crude. (*Explains*.) She's always telling me that I say crude things.

KEITH: It's okay. My Mom says that we should talk about death.

LISA: I agree.

BRIAN: Your Mom also reads her horoscope every day. (*Keith crosses to Lisa and continues on with his story.*)

KEITH: His name was Kirk. Real good lookin' guy. Best surfer I ever knew. That's why everybody was so blown away when they heard.

LISA: I don't know much about surfing, but I would think that they were good swimmers.

KEITH: They think maybe his board smacked him on the head or somethin'...that happens to the best of them. The Coronary guy...

BRIAN: Coroner.

KEITH: Right. He said it was hard to tell because the body got banged up pretty bad before it rolled up on shore.

LISA: So what do you think happened?

KEITH: Personally, I think the undercurrent pulled him out. It was night and kinda stormy. He was just out too far and couldn't make it in.

LISA: He went surfing at night?

KEITH: Yeah. Kirk was like that. Always livin' on the edge. One dangerous dude.

CONNIE: Were you with him when it happened?

BRIAN: No.

KEITH: Some jogger found him. Ocean just kinda spit him up on the shore. (*Pause.*) I've seen dead seals, dogs, even saw a dead baby whale once...but I never saw a real body here before. Sure glad I wasn't the one that found him.

LISA: Was he all bloated and stuff?

KEITH: Don't know...they made him look pretty good for the funeral. It was open-casket.

LISA: Really?

CONNIE: Lisa, I don't think you should pry into this. It's kinda personal.

KEITH: It's okay. I don't mind.

BRIAN: Yeah, well I do. (*Brian takes a few steps away from them in total disgust. Lisa ignores him and crosses to Keith.*)

LISA: Connie knew a guy who had his head cut off in a car accident.

CONNIE: Lisa!

KEITH: Whoa...all the way off?

LISA: It took the police over an hour to find it.

KEITH: That's bizarre.

LISA: And when they did find it, the guy had this expression on his face. Ya know, like it was frozen in a scream.

KEITH: That's intense.

LISA: Bet that guy didn't have an open casket.

KEITH: It really makes you stop and think. Kirk drowned. Her friend was decapulated. I mean...we're all gonna die, but we never know how or when.

LISA: I hope I go out quick when I die.

KEITH: Me too. That's one good thing...at least Kirk didn't have to suffer.

BRIAN: How do you know he didn't suffer?

LISA: What's his problem?

CONNIE: Lisa, these guys just lost a close friend. Don't start anything.

KEITH: She's not startin' anything. I think we should talk about it. (*Brian turns back to Keith.*)

BRIAN: With strangers?

KEITH: My Mom says people can talk about things with strangers easier than with people they know.

LISA: I've heard that, too. (*Keith crosses to Brian.*)

KEITH: Kirk's gone, Brian. And right now I need to talk about that. And I don't think it's fair that you're giving me a hard time.

BRIAN: Fair? I'll tell you what's not fair, my friend. That Kirk left me behind to explain... (*Brian stops himself.*)

KEITH: Explain? Explain what?

BRIAN: You're way out of line here, Keith.

KEITH: I'm out of line?

BRIAN: You don't understand?

KEITH: You're right, I don't understand.

CONNIE: Look, maybe we should go. (*There is a tense moment as Keith and Brian stare at each other.*)

LISA: Connie's right. We should go...we have to get her foot checked out.

KEITH: She's just gonna get the cut all dirty.

CONNIE: I'll be all right. (*Connie gets up and tries to walk on her cut foot; winces from the pain, but tries not to let it show.*)

KEITH: Oh no you don't. (*He crosses to her and sits her back down on the incline.*)

KEITH: The Life Guard Headquarters isn't too far from here...I'll head over there and see if they got some spare bandages. (*Bragging.*) Happen to be pretty tight with those guys.

CONNIE: I thought you said this was off season?

KEITH: It is, but there's always a couple of them around. Usually the old ones. They don't do much 'cept suck up coffee all day.

LISA: Hot coffee...that sounds so good right now.

KEITH: You can come with me...but you better leave the mouse ears here. Hangin' with a tourist could ruin my reputation.

LISA: Yeah, right. (*She takes off her mouse ears and tosses them to Connie.*)

CONNIE: I'll guard them with my life.

KEITH: (*To Brian:*) You don't mind stayin' here?

BRIAN: Just don't take all day.

CONNIE: Remember, Lisa...We're supposed to be back by five.

KEITH: It's not very far. We shouldn't be more than ten minutes.

LISA: Connie, we're doing this all for you. keith looks down the coastline.

KEITH: Damn, high tide is startin' to come in. I hate walkin' in mush. (*Keith heads off, Lisa runs after him. There is an awkward* *moment of silence between Brian and Connie. Finally...)*

CONNIE: I always feel like her Mother the way I have to get after her about things.

BRIAN: I can relate. (*Pause.*)

CONNIE: You really don't have to babysit me...I'll be alright.

BRIAN: They won't be long. Besides, I don't really feel like going home yet. (*Pause.*)

CONNIE: I'm really sorry about your friend, Kirk. The last thing you need right now is a couple of tourists from the midwest bothering you.

BRIAN: I don't have any problem with tourists. That's Keith. And even he doesn't really believe it...it's kind of a game with him. (*Pause.*) To tell you the truth, he's swollen for Lisa.

CONNIE: Swollen?

BRIAN: Beach term. He likes Lisa.

CONNIE: Swollen. That's cute.

BRIAN: Something for you to take back home.

CONNIE: It might make up for my lack of tan.

BRIAN: Just tell them you used sunblock.

CONNIE: You talking about skin lotion...or the weather here?

BRIAN: That's a good question.

CONNIE: Oh well, even a bad day in California beats a great day in Ohio.

BRIAN: If I was in a little better frame of mind...I'd show you some of the local sights.

CONNIE: You've got enough to think about right now.

BRIAN: Maybe in a couple of days. When do you go back?

CONNIE: Tomorrow.

BRIAN: So much for that idea.

CONNIE: Our plane leaves at six in the morning. I think our parents planned that. We'll be so tired that we won't protest.

BRIAN: Most of my friends can't wait to get *out* of Los Angeles.

CONNIE: That's because you live here.

BRIAN: Probably.

CONNIE: We're thinking of coming back next year. We only got a week and couldn't see everything.

BRIAN: That's what happens when you travel with your parents.

CONNIE: Right. (*Pause. Brian catches himself staring at her.*)

BRIAN: Uh..so, how's your foot?

CONNIE: Better.

BRIAN: That's good.

CONNIE: I can't believe I stepped on that glass. It was so stupid of me.

BRIAN: Keith cut his foot on a soda can last month. And that's a lot easier to spot than a piece of glass.

CONNIE: Soda?

BRIAN: Soda...you know, Coke, Pepsi...7-UP.

CONNIE: Oh...Pop.

BRIAN: What?

CONNIE: We call it pop...soda pop.

BRIAN: Pop...very strange.

CONNIE: Well whatever...I should have been looking where I was going. I guess I was too busy looking at the beautiful scenery.

BRIAN: That's California alright...one big picture postcard.

CONNIE: It's the palm trees. They're so exotic. This place is...paradise.

BRIAN: Paradise. (*Brian looks out at the ocean.*)

CONNIE: It must be neat living so near the Ocean. You can come down here anytime you want.

BRIAN: And the repetition of the waves
and the simple sand
and the screaming seagulls
circle round me
like a tornado
and I stand in the center
completely untouched
but not unmoved.

CONNIE: You're a poet?

BRIAN: Not me. Kirk wrote that. The poem was called "Paradise."

CONNIE: It's very good.

BRIAN: You're the first one to hear it. Other than myself.

CONNIE: Really?

BRIAN: Kirk kept his feelings a secret from most people. Thought it was easier if everyone just thought of him as a waterlogged surf boy.

CONNIE: He sure had a way with words.

BRIAN: I told him he should do something with his writing. You know...turn it into something. But he only wrote when it pleased him.

CONNIE: Most artists are like that.

BRIAN: He was an artist all right. (*She notices that Brian is staring off; deep in thought. There is a moment of silence.*)

CONNIE: Listen, I feel real awkward here.

BRIAN: So do I.

CONNIE: You need some time alone. To sort all of this out.

BRIAN: I've had too much time alone.

CONNIE: If you want me to go...just say so. I'll understand.

BRIAN: What are you gonna do? Crawl back to your hotel?

CONNIE: I'm not hurt that bad. Besides, I feel a little guilty. I'm holding you hostage here.

BRIAN: Actually I like talking with you.

CONNIE: I just wish I could be better support. (*Pause.*) I mean, I didn't know your friend.

BRIAN: Nobody really knew Kirk. They only knew what he let them know.

CONNIE: My Dad is like that. Keeps everything inside.

BRIAN: I wish Kirk would have been like that with me. But for some unknown reason, I became the ear...he told me everything. (*More to himself:*) Almost everything.

CONNIE: Everyone needs someone they can confide in. I know I do.

BRIAN: He would tell me things like his poetry, but wouldn't listen to my advice. It was very frustrating.

CONNIE: I can understand that.

BRIAN: It's like he trusted me, but only to a point. I remember once we had to write a poem for English Class...Kirk was already way behind in the homework department and if he didn't turn this one in it would have meant flunking for sure. All he had to do was to turn in one of his poems, but he wouldn't.

CONNIE: What happened?

BRIAN: I turned it in for him. Took it out of his notebook in our locker and dropped it off, along with mine.

CONNIE: So he passed?

BRIAN: Barely. Kirk didn't talk to me for a week. To this day I still can't understand why he was so upset about that.

CONNIE: You were just trying to help.

BRIAN: I guess he would rather have failed than to let someone know he was sensitive. (*Pause.*) He always told me "If you don't show your cards to people, they can't beat your hand."

CONNIE: But you could also say that if you don't show your cards, you can't win the game. (*Brian looks at her in amazement.*)

BRIAN: I don't believe you just said that.

CONNIE: I'm sorry. I didn't mean to...

BRIAN: No, don't be sorry. I said the same thing to him. The very same thing.

CONNIE: Really? (*Long Pause.*)

BRIAN: He bought a new surfboard last week. Used the money he was saving for college. He didn't need a new board...already had three of the best and a big company was talking to him about sponsorship. But he just got up one day and decided to buy another one. (*Pause.*) It was the last one he ever rode.

CONNIE: That's sad.

BRIAN: The day before he died, I stopped at his house after school. He missed two days in a row and I was going to give him the old "no diploma, no surf tour" speech. He just laughed it off. (*Pause.*) We came down here and I watched as he broke in his new board. Rolling, shooting, pitching back and forth. The guy was incredible. Perfect balance. He had so much talent. (*Pause.*) We sat for an hour and talked about his upcoming tournament. Girls. School. The usual stuff. (*Breaking a bit.*) And I said to myself...I've never seen Kirk so happy. But he wasn't. There was something inside of him that was tearing him up. And I just don't understand why he couldn't have talked to me about it. Instead of letting it push him over the edge.

CONNIE: Over the edge?

BRIAN: Kirk's drowning was no accident. He committed suicide. (*There is a moment of silence. Connie is a bit awkward with this new information. Brian pulls a letter from his jacket.*) The day after he died, I found this letter in our locker at school. (*Angry.*) Didn't leave it with his Mom, or his girlfriend...no, he chose me to be the one to find it.

CONNIE: You sure you want to tell me this? I mean, it was pretty obvious that Keith wants people to think it was an accident.

BRIAN: That's because Keith thinks it was.

CONNIE: You haven't told him yet?

BRIAN: I haven't told anyone. Except you. (*Connie looks at him for a moment.*)

CONNIE: Why?

BRIAN: I don't know.

CONNIE: Not even his parents?

Brad Slaight

BRIAN: Especially not them. (*Connie is not sure what she should say. Decides to say nothing.*)

BRIAN: When I read his letter, my first impulse was to run to his parents. But I just kinda walked around for a few hours. And then when I went to the funeral home that night and saw them all there...crying and talking about how great of a kid he was... (*Brian breaks a bit. He takes a few steps away.*)

BRIAN: Goddamn him for doing this to me. For doing this to everyone. (*Pause.*)

CONNIE: I don't know what to say.

BRIAN: And neither did I. So I just didn't say anything. (*Pause.*)

BRIAN: What would you have done?

CONNIE: I don't know. I can see how hard it would be. I mean, it's not the kind of thing people would want to hear. But sooner or later they would have to be told.

BRIAN: Today at the funeral, I wanted to stand up in the middle of the service and just scream it out...you know, take care of it all at once. And then I looked around at the faces. And I heard the crying again. When a young person dies the crying is always louder...more painful.

CONNIE: Well I can understand how that wouldn't have been the place...

BRIAN: I even thought about not telling anyone...ever. He's dead. This can only hurt the ones who are already in pain. If I never said anything...at least they wouldn't have to go through what I'm going through. Maybe it's best just to keep it to myself.

CONNIE: But you're telling me.

BRIAN: It just came out. Maybe Keith's Mother was right...maybe it is easier to talk to strangers. (*Brian looks at Connie for a moment.*)

BRIAN: God, I'm sorry. This really isn't fair to dump on you.

CONNIE: It's alright. I understand.

BRIAN: But you didn't know Kirk. And you don't know me. It's just that...well I had to tell somebody. (*Pause.*) I thought I could tell Keith...I thought if we came down here, away from all of those people, I'd show him the letter and talk with him about it...but every time I tried, the words seemed to choke up in my throat.

CONNIE: He could help you get through this.

BRIAN: Keith looked up to Kirk. We all did. Something like this...what if he decides to do the same thing? What if it pushes him over the edge, too? (*Brian turns away and faces the ocean.*)

BRIAN: They're going to blame me for what happened to Kirk.

CONNIE: Why would anyone blame you?

BRIAN: Because I didn't see it coming. I knew him better than anyone else. I should have known.

CONNIE: But you didn't.

BRIAN: Why couldn't he have given me a clue? Some kind of sign. Even his letter...doesn't really say why. (*Reads from letter.*) "Brian, By the time you get this letter I will be dead. I'm sorry for putting you through this. I can't go on. Kirk." (*Pause.*) Can't go on? What the hell is that supposed to mean? Why couldn't he have gone on? Why?

CONNIE: There's nothing you could have done.

BRIAN: I keep going over and over the last time I saw him. Trying to remember everything we talked about...something he said that might have been a clue. But there was nothing. (*Pause.*) He kept everything inside...and he took it all with him.

CONNIE: And if you do the game thing...you've learned nothing from his mistake. (*Quickly.*) I'm sorry...I shouldn't have said that.

BRIAN: Don't be sorry.

CONNIE: But I have no right to criticize you. I mean, I have no idea what you're going through right now. (*We hear the sound of a siren, approaching quickly. Brian looks down the coastline and realizes it's coming their way.*)

CONNIE: What's going on?

BRIAN: Lifeguard.

CONNIE: Listen, whatever you've told me...it's strictly between you and me.

BRIAN: Thanks. (*We hear the siren very close. Then it shuts off. Followed by the sound of a truck door shutting. Keith enters and does not appear very happy. He is followed by Lisa and a young, well built lifeguard who carries a medical kit.*)

LISA: She's over here...right over here. (*She scurries over to Connie.*)

LISA: Look what I found. A gen-u-ine California hunk.

KEITH: Old Morey's on vacation this month.

LISA: His name is Tony. (*Keith shoots Brian a look of disgust at her infatuation with Tony, who is now looking at Connie's foot.*)

TONY: I thought you said your friend broke her leg.

LISA: (*Playful.*) Did I?

CONNIE: Whatta you think, Doc? Am I gonna live?

TONY: It's just a minor laceration. I'm going to clean it out...put some disinfectant on it.

LISA: These lifeguards sure know there business.

KEITH: I coulda done that.

LISA: Then why didn't you?

KEITH: Cause I didn't have a bag a' supplies like junior here.

TONY: Junior?

KEITH: Well you are kinda young to be a lifeguard.

TONY: For your information, I happen to have over four years experience as a lifeguard. And on beaches a heck of a lot more dangerous than this.

LISA: Yeah...so back off.

KEITH: Well, it's a real shame you weren't here the other night when my friend went down.

TONY: You mean the surfer?

KEITH: Yeah...where were you guys?

CONNIE: (*Breaking the tension.*) Hey, I thought he was here to help me. Do you mind, we've got to get back to our hotel. (*Tony crosses over to Connie and starts to wrap up her foot.*)

LISA: Doesn't Tony have a great tan, Connie? I'd kill to go back home lookin' like him. (*Tony finishes up and starts to close up his bag.*)

TONY: That oughta hold you for now. I suggest you keep an eye on it and if it shows any sign of infection see your doctor.

CONNIE: Thanks for the disclaimer.

TONY: Part of the job.

LISA: Tony, do you think you can give us a ride up to our hotel? It's just a little ways from here, near the Pier.

KEITH: I already told you...we'll give you a ride.

LISA: But your car is way over in the parking lot. His truck is right here.

Brad Slaight

TONY: I guess I could give you a ride.

LISA: Did you hear that, Connie? He said he'd give us a ride.

CONNIE: It's my foot that's hurt, not my ears. (*Tony crosses over to Keith.*)

TONY: Listen, I'm really sorry about your buddy. And to tell you the truth, I wish I would have been here.

BRIAN: It's not your fault. (*Brian shoots a look to Keith.*)

KEITH: Alright, I guess I was out of line.

TONY: I'm kinda new here. Sure don't want to get off on the wrong foot with the locals. We may need each other some day. (*He holds out his hand to Keith. Keith looks at tony for a moment; then accepts his handshake.*)

KEITH: Yeah, okay. But I do have one suggestion.

TONY: What's that?

KEITH: Don't dress so trendy, bro'. Save it for when you're assigned down Malibu way.

TONY: I'll make a note of that. (*Connie slowly stands up. She hobbles over to Brian.*)

CONNIE: Do you want me to stay?

BRIAN: No. I'll be all right. (*She takes a piece of paper out of her purse and scribbles something.*)

CONNIE: Here's my phone number. Use it or lose it. I'll understand either way.

LISA: Connie...come on.

CONNIE: Well, I better go.

BRIAN: Thanks, Connie. Don't take this wrong, but I'm real glad you cut your foot.

CONNIE: So am I. (*Brian kisses Connie. She holds for a moment and then hobbles over to Tony and a very stunned Lisa. Keith crosses over to Brian.*)

TONY: If you guys want, I'll drop you off at your car on the way.

KEITH: (*To Brian.*) We should probably head out. I promised Mrs. Woodman we'd stop by the house.

BRIAN: Go ahead.

KEITH: (*A bit hurt.*) Yeah...well, later. (*Keith turns and starts to walk towards the others, who are starting to leave.*)

BRIAN: Keith...wait. (*Keith stops.*)

KEITH: What?

BRIAN: Don't go...Please. (*Connie indicates that she, Lisa and Tony should leave. They do. Long Pause. Interrupted only by the sound of the truck being driven away.*)

KEITH: Look, man...I'm sorry about before. If you need time alone...hey...I understand.

BRIAN: No. I don't want to be alone right now. And you don't either. (*Brian crosses to keith and puts his arm around him. Brian leads him back to the edge of the ocean and they both sit.*)

KEITH: Can you believe that girl, Lisa?

BRIAN: Not your type?

KEITH: She's a turdist.

BRIAN: Right.

KEITH: You swollen for Connie?

BRIAN: I don't know. (*They both look out at the ocean for a long* *moment.)*

KEITH: Gonna be a high tide again tonight.

BRIAN: Really?

KEITH: Seven, maybe even an eight.

BRIAN: That is high.

KEITH: If this keeps up, we're not gonna have much beach left.

BRIAN: Never liked the stormy season...makes the beach seem so empty.

KEITH: It'll be over soon. long pause.

BRIAN: The tide rolls in
pressing down the surrendering sand
which doesn't seem to mind
and then
without warning
the tide rolls back out
to hide among the waves
leaving behind
a simple reminder
that it will return again.

KEITH: Did Kirk write that? (*The same song as we heard in the opening begins to play, only this time it's not played from the tape deck and not quite so loud.*

The lights fade so that Brian and Keith are in silhouette.)

THE END

VOICES
from
Young Actors

What follows are excerpts from the writing of six of the young actors who worked on the first productions of these plays. At A.C.T., we encourage young actors to articulate their acting experiences by writing both during and after a project. Some of these actors were in more than one of the new plays and have comparative experiences. Age and background also condition their feelings about the process. As we have seen, each playwright utilizes a process that is specific to their manner and that this process varies (sometimes greatly) from playwright to playwright, offering different perspectives for both players and the audience. The ages listed with the actor's names are the ages at the time of their writing.

DEVON ANGUS
Age 17
Played Rafe in *Windshook* and Pop in *Reindeer Soup*

There is a specific glory in a line spoken for the first time. It's a special secret for the actor, different from all of the other lines spoken by him before because he owns it. For the rest of time, he owns it, no matter how many other actors will say the line in the future, it remains a birth. The actor speaking lines from a new play for the first time experiences the birth of a character, one more living and breathing character to be added to the history of the theater. It may not be remembered, but it is yours.

There is a sizable risk in staging a new play. As in any play the other actors may not know each other, may feel intimidated by the play or the role, the actors and director may or may not get along...the possibilities are frightening. A new play brings in the playwright, rewrites, the insecurity of not having tested the play yet in front of an audience. In spite all of that, there is a fire that enters you everytime you walk into that rehearsal space. There is a spontaneity in the words, a sensitivity to the writing that, with each rewrite, brings the images of your character more and more into focus. You acquire a deep respect for the playwright and these characters that you have embraced. And your words sink into the script, and get stirred up and mixed in with the words of the directors and the playwrights and the other actors until the result is a true collaboration, a script with a little piece of everybody in it.

When working on something like this, you begin to lose yourself in the play. Everyone works so closely and so hard, there is a bond that holds everyone together throughout the rehearsals and the performances that is really much stronger than family. It is such a personal experience for everyone involved. It is a shame that finally you take off your costume and make your return to reality, leaving behind everything you worked so hard for. But it remains inside of you, that person you created and lived, and for a short time you are the only one who ever lived that role. It's having added to the future of the theater that is your reward.

I was twice a part of this moving, thinking, breathing, process. I had the experience of being actor and collaborator. I have such respect for the Timothy Masons, and the Mary Gallaghers, and the Joe Pintauros, and the Brad Slaights who have written these human plays about young people. As Mr. Pintauro said, "We all will remember this for the rest of our lives." I have, and I will.

ANDREW IRONS
Age 17
Played Jerry in *Ascension Day* and Dylan/Pop in *Windshook*

Never before have I ever had an experience quite like the one I had in the summer of 1990. I feel extremely lucky that I had the opportunity to work on new plays with professional playwrights. I came to the American Conservatory Theater knowing that I had a lot to learn and experience, and I left with the thought that I would never fully satisfy my curiosity about the theater. That summer changed my mind about what I was doing in the theater, because I had the chance to be a part of the building process. I was able to see just how much creativity is involved with bringing a new play to life. To see how a play was pieced together from the beginning, and then be a part of the final product was an experience that very few people my age will ever have. Having the playwright with us, I was now able to see what development was necessary in order to create a character properly.

There have been so many times that I have been put into a role that I knew nothing about. *Ascension Day* and *Windshook* gave me roles that I could really relate to. I felt I could understand these characters from my own personal experience. I feel very fortunate to have been a part of these two plays.

ADELA LACZYNSKI
Age 12
Played Julie in *Reindeer Soup*

I had been studying acting at A.C.T. for a year when I was asked to play Julie in *Reindeer Soup*. The work on the play was both a class (Performance Workshop) and a production. It was, at first, difficult to explain this to my friends. How can you learn acting *and* do a play? I wasn't exactly sure how it would work myself. As we began rehearsals, it seemed clearer to me. We were learning acting in the best possible way — actually rehearsing a play to perform in front of an audience. And there was the added excitement of working on a brand new play — with the playwright.

In the beginning, I wasn't sure how to play Julie. She's my age but the circumstances are so different than my life. She has a long speech about protecting animals. It is an emotional statement. I didn't know how to do that speech. But having Joe Pintauro, the man who wrote the speech, at rehearsals was helpful. He helped me so much in bringing my character to life. We were all nervous having the playwright actually with us. We all thought, he'll hate us! But then he was so nice. After Joe explained that Julie was hallucinating in an especially difficult scene, I began to understand the character.

I hope that I'll be able to experience again a class and a play in my training. I had so much fun participating in *Reindeer Soup* -- being the first actor to play Julie -- and I'm so sorry it's over.

SHONA MITCHELL
Age 16
Played Julie in *Windshook*

I remember walking into the room, slightly out of breath after the climb up three flights of familiar stairs, on the first day of rehearsal. I recognized a few faces from previous classes at A.C.T., and the remainder I was sure I'd get to know soon enough. We began by introducing ourselves and did a quick read through. The script was only halfway done, about twenty pages, but we were informed that we would be getting bits and pieces in the next few weeks. We also learned that we would meet Mary Gallagher, the playwright, and work with her for two weeks.

When Mary arrived from New York, the first thing she had us do was close our eyes and listen to an old Scottish song, "The Mill o' Tifty's Annie." She told us that that song was the inspiration behind the play we were working on. We then began discussing the play with her. Since the play was not yet finished, we all put in our own thoughts as to what we think would happen at the end, and she took our suggestions.

The whole process was much different than any other play I had worked on before. Being able to work with Mary for two weeks was really fun for me, and for her too, I'm sure. It was really interesting to see the play progress as the weeks went on. We were always full of questions and she was always ready to answer them. I don't think I have ever seen a group of young actors work so well together before. I think one of the main reasons is that we were not treated as children, but with respect, which gave us a lot more room to move and grow. Everybody became so close in the few weeks we had, it was amazing. We worked very hard together, with only five weeks to get the show up, but we always found a way to have fun. Even outside of rehearsal we went to concerts together and had a great time.

Those five weeks went by so quickly, I was sad to see *Windshook* go up. Towards the end of our last performance, as I was sitting in the back of the studio, I began to cry. Part of the reason was the actual end of the play itself, but mostly it was because I realized that after tonight, it would all be over. All the friends I had made, all the fun we had, all the hard work was now finally paying off. It was a beautiful feeling, but at the same time, almost heartbreaking.

PAUL SCHIKANY
Age 17
Played Charlie in *Reindeer Soup* and Brian in *High Tide*

The opportunity to take part in a new play is an exciting one for any actor. The process of creating a new character, literally breathing life into a character, and knowing that you are the first one to do so, would have to rank highly with any individual. I have had the privilege of working on two such plays, *High Tide*, by Brad Slaight, and *Reindeer Soup*, by Joe Pintauro. The experiences have been inspiring and memorable for me, and I am grateful for the honor of working on them.

The process of creating a new play was unique, in that many interesting elements were added to the rehearsal process. The script revisions added an unusual twist to line memorization. Entire pages of dialogue were frequently changed, leading to curious "flashbacks," where an actor would suddenly recite a line that had been deleted long ago. Mr. Pintauro's presence during rehearsals of *Reindeer Soup* became a greatly appreciated aid in interpretation of the script. He provided useful insights into the character's lives, and became a close friend to the cast.

These plays have been an invaluable part of my training as an actor. To any actor with an opportunity to work on a new play, I urge you to go for it! The memories will last forever, and the rewards are innumerable.

DAWNN STEEVES
Age 18
Played Iona in *Reindeer Soup*

(note: Dawnn kept a journal throughout the rehearsal period What follows are selected entries from that journal)

Wednesday, July 22, 1992: Well, there's no going back now. The first rehearsal is over. I don't know if I should feel overwhelmed with excitement or fear. There is a lot of pressure in being the first cast to perform a play. However, after meeting the cast and reading thru the script a few times I feel confident that everything is going to work out.

As always the first rehearsal was rather quiet for the actors. Craig (the Director) did most of the talking. It is comforting to know he has researched the play extensively, and has a vision and a direction for us to take. However, I won't believe the 24 point buck reindeer until I see it.

The script is great. It is so refreshing to see youth presented as multi-dimensional humans, rather than the typical flat single minded characters we are accustomed to portraying over and over again. At the same time, each character has an equally significant role in the play. There are no leads. This will be a true ensemble piece.

Well, enough for now. I had better get back to memorizing lines and figuring out more about how to be a mystical, feminist, Eskimo.

Monday, July 27: Today we got out of our seats and into our characters. We worked on improvisation that required us to understand our personal objectives and relationships with the other character. These exercises helped me to shake off Dawn. It's exciting to watch each of the characters develop personal traits and come into an existence of their own. This seems to make everything real and alive. We basically started a sort of free staging today, where the actors were guided by their impulses from the script, with added guidance from Craig. This allowed for self-discovery and made the motivation for movement. At one point during rehearsal, Pop and Chrissie were sitting at the table during a scene between Vince and Charlie. During the scene, Chrissie did some kind of movement with Pop, an interchange that wasn't really in the play but a distracted game between the two actors. Craig stopped the scene, encouraged the two actors to actually play the game (ROCK - PAPER - SCISSORS) and started the scene again. Watching from the seats while the scene was repeated I was delighted by the new interaction, how appropriate it seemed that a mentally off-balanced father would tune out the serious matters of the two boys were talking about and tune into a simple game of ROCK-PAPER-SCISSORS with all of his competitive energy. Not only did it make me laugh, but it made me believe that the father was a close part of the children's lives. This obviously was not the first time such a game had been played between father and child.

Friday, August 7: What a privilege, to actually sit face to face with your character's creator! Today we had the opportunity to officially meet Joe Pintauro and ask questions. What was the relationship between Mom and Iona? I didn't ask this question but it had been on my mind since the first read thru. Mr. Pintauro offered me a million connections by simply talking about how Mom represented the past, like the fifties, when everything was good, wholesome and happy. And how the children and Pop live in the present, where the "American Dream" is dead. Iona is part of a future new world. Iona is mystical. He described her as being like the Blessed Virgin Mary, a redeemer. She is a part of divine destiny. She is upset that Norman (the reindeer) was killed, but she knows it was for a reason. She has to juggle and balance herself between these two factors. She is the redeemer and passes out the "communion" (the bowls of soup). I was also interested in knowing more about the final moment for Iona when Chrissie calls her "Mom." As we were discussing the exchange between the characters, Joe began to play with the idea that Iona might reply to "Mom" with "No." This may or may not change, but it still sent shivers down my spine. One, because the alteration of a single phrase completely escalated the intensity of the entire scene. Two, watching the wheels of a playwright's mind turn as he made decisions that affected the entire production was amazing.

Monday, August 10: Today, I had an interview with an actress who has taught theater to eskimo children. We thought she could provide some insights into my character. She really was helpful. Eskimos do not use a lot of hand gestures when they speak. They value the community over the individual, everything is for the group. They have an intense respect for the land and the animals which inhabit it. They believe that if they are good or do not pray before and after "the kill," the animals will go away. Tradition is very important. I have made some important physical decisions for Iona.

Back to rehearsal. NEW SCRIPTS!!! Wow, Joe Pintauro revised the script over the weekend, lots of minor changes, new lines and tightening up. Things are more clear now. Characters seem to be more defined. Guess what? Iona was given an entire new background with one new line, "That's not accurate, I'm from Kentucky originally." I have specific choices to make now. Iona with an attitude.

Rehearsal was scary today. We have only two weeks left and we're still using scripts. The first scene is dragging tremendously. Some of the actors seem to be "acting." Joe Pintauro doesn't look very happy. Energy needs to increase. I am starting to get a little bit nervous.

Wednesday, August 12: We really made some progress today. We started with Mom's scene and went through to the end with directions from Craig. Then we ran it again on our own and then Craig gave notes. It really helped a lot to feel continuity. I have never been dependent on a script this far into rehearsals and this close to performance time. Probably the most helpful thing for me today was a private rehearsal with Craig in which we really went through my entire role. We cleared up questions and I made my intentions and interpretations concrete. As an actor, it will now be easier for me to commit to my movements and attitudes moment to moment. I feel I have a strong base now to really start building upon. The hardest part is over for me now. I know Iona!

JOE PINTAURO'S LAST DAY IN CALIFORNIA,

August 15: What a thrill, the process of being a part of a living art. It is not as if we are trapped in a frame like a painting. We are continually blooming outwards. There are no limitations to our relationships as playwright, director, manager, actor or audience. We are all humans filled with passion and a common desire to teach fellow humans to see the world in a different light.

Watching Joe Pintauro stumble over words in his head, deciding how to add lines and rephrases some of Julie and Iona's words, reminded me of God in the Book of Genesis when he put his lips to Adam and gave him his first breath. Such an intimate relationship. God didn't just throw a lightening bolt from atop a mountain high. No, he went down and formed him with his own breath. This same bond exists between playwright and character. At times I was almost embarrassed to watch Joe add dimensions to his characters. It's like stumbling into a room with two people kissing.

My goal as an actress is to receive that breath of air that makes me real.

PERMISSIONS ACKNOWLEDGMENTS